Coffee Table Books 3D

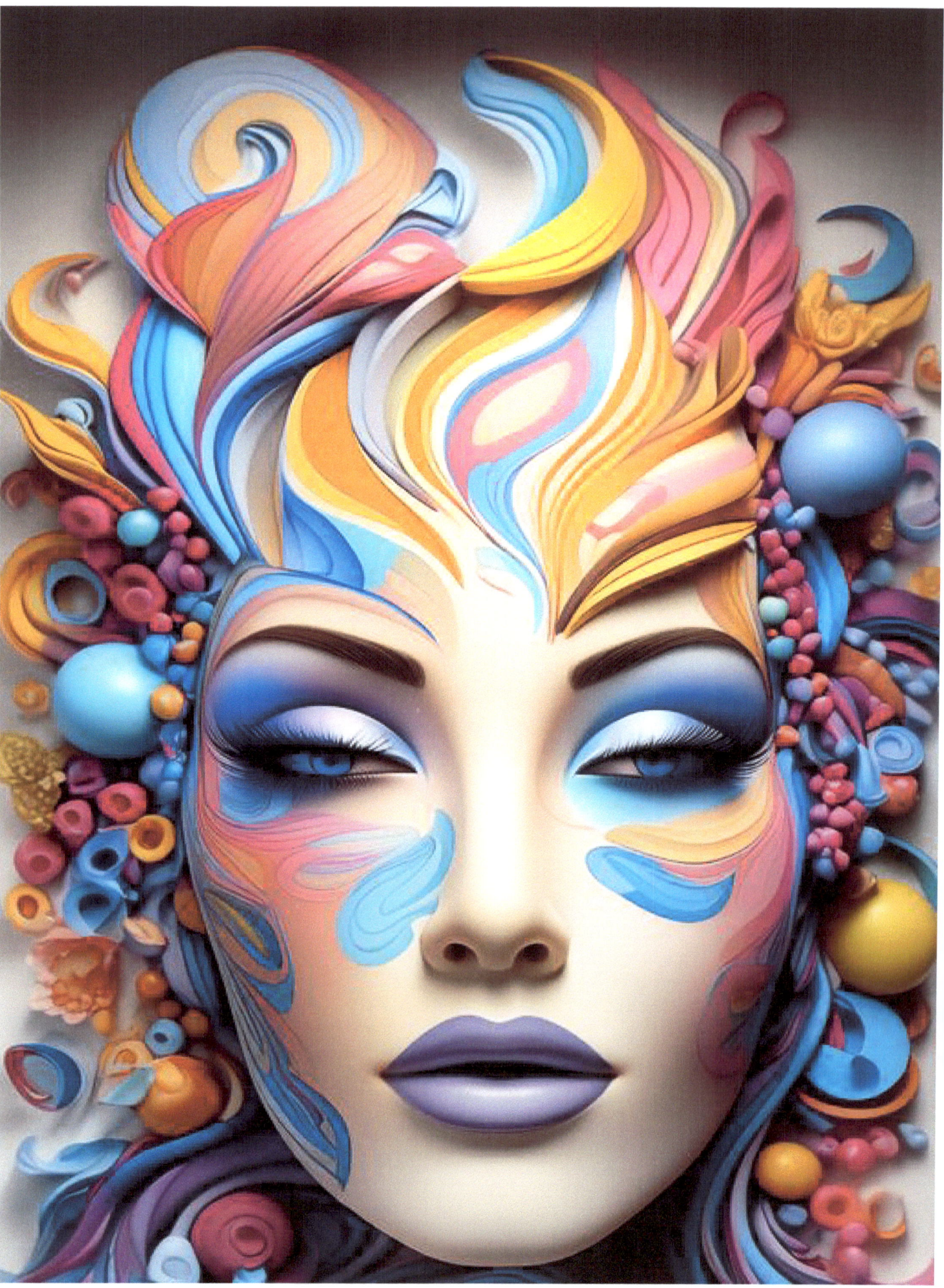

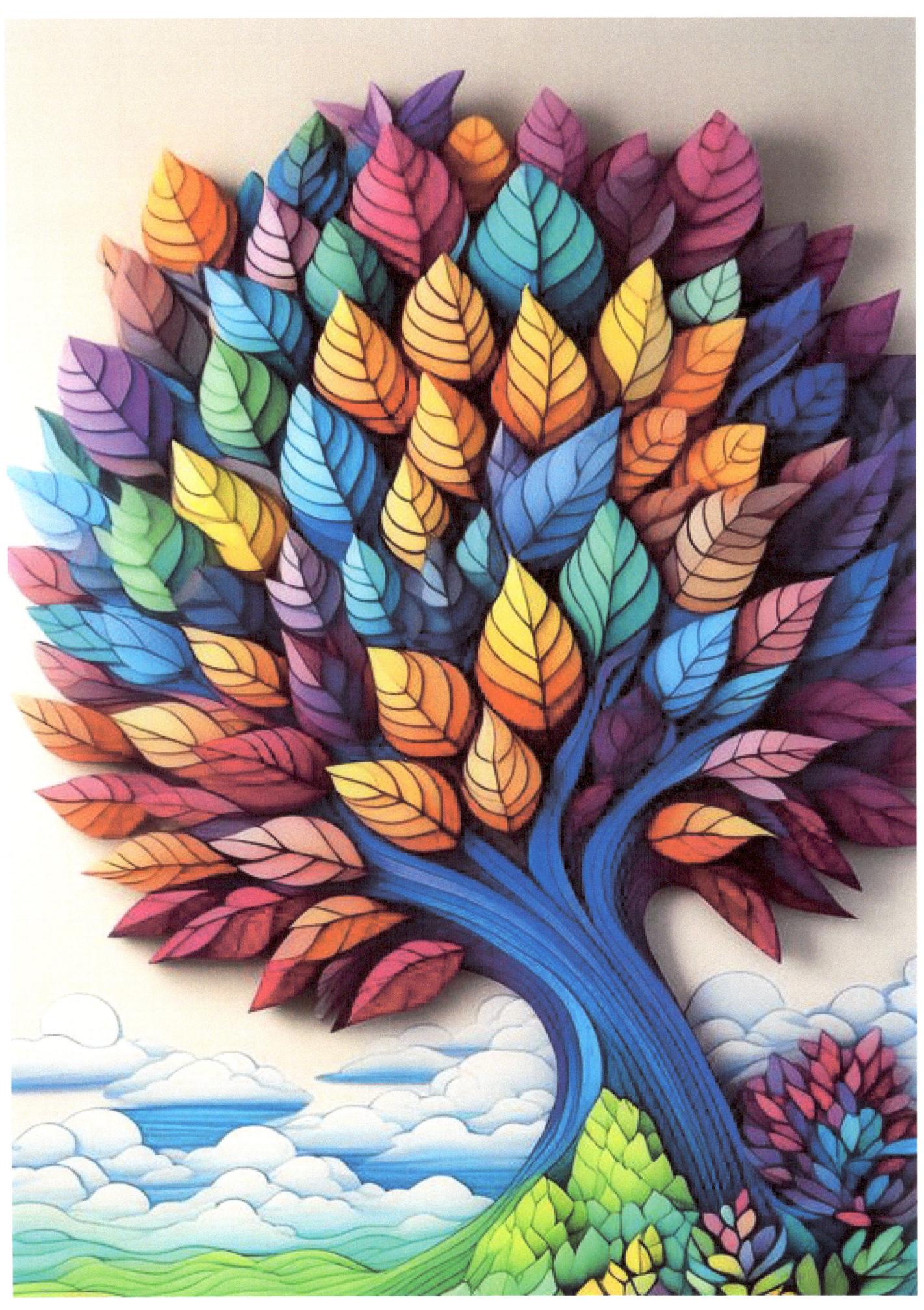

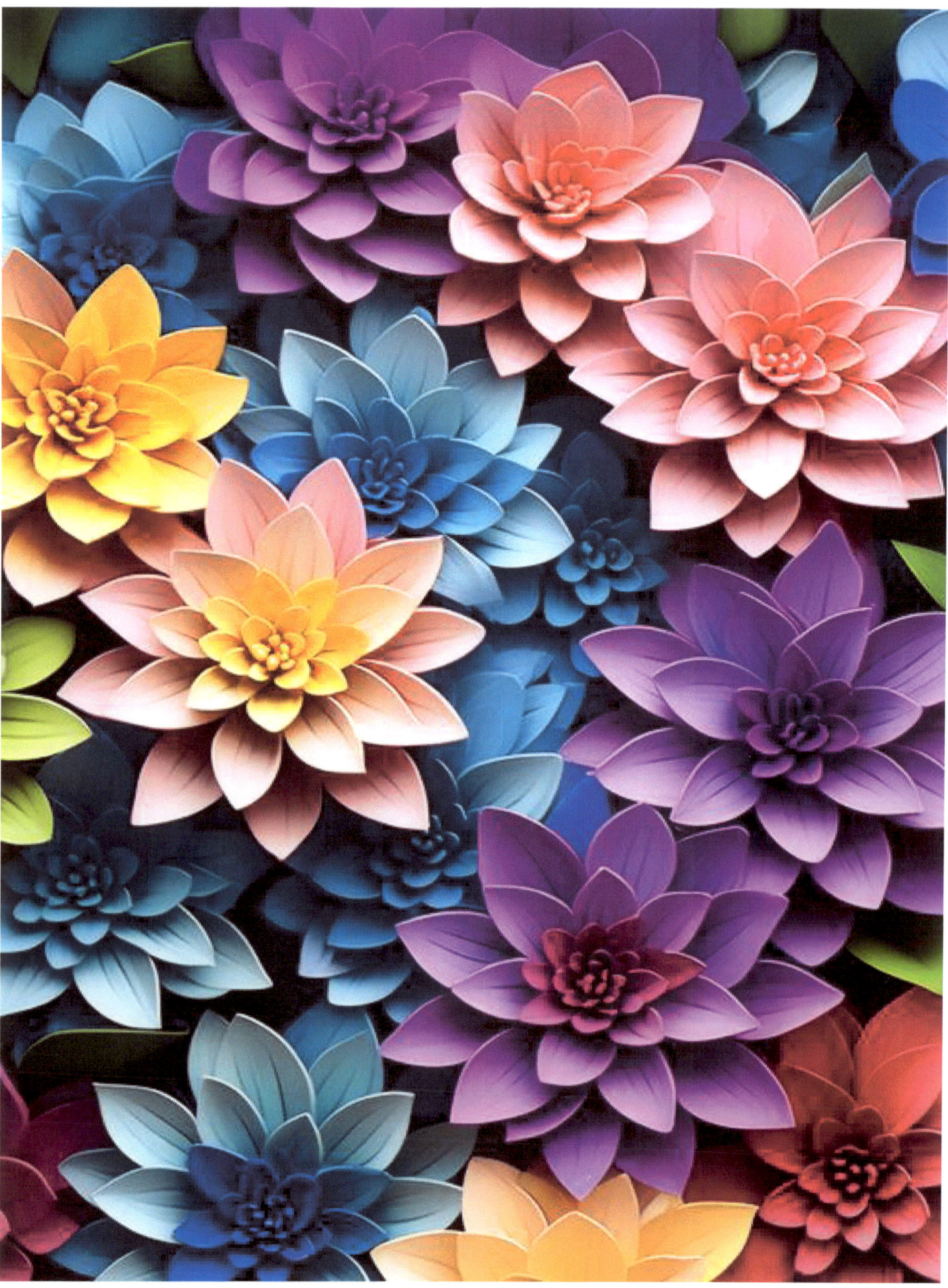

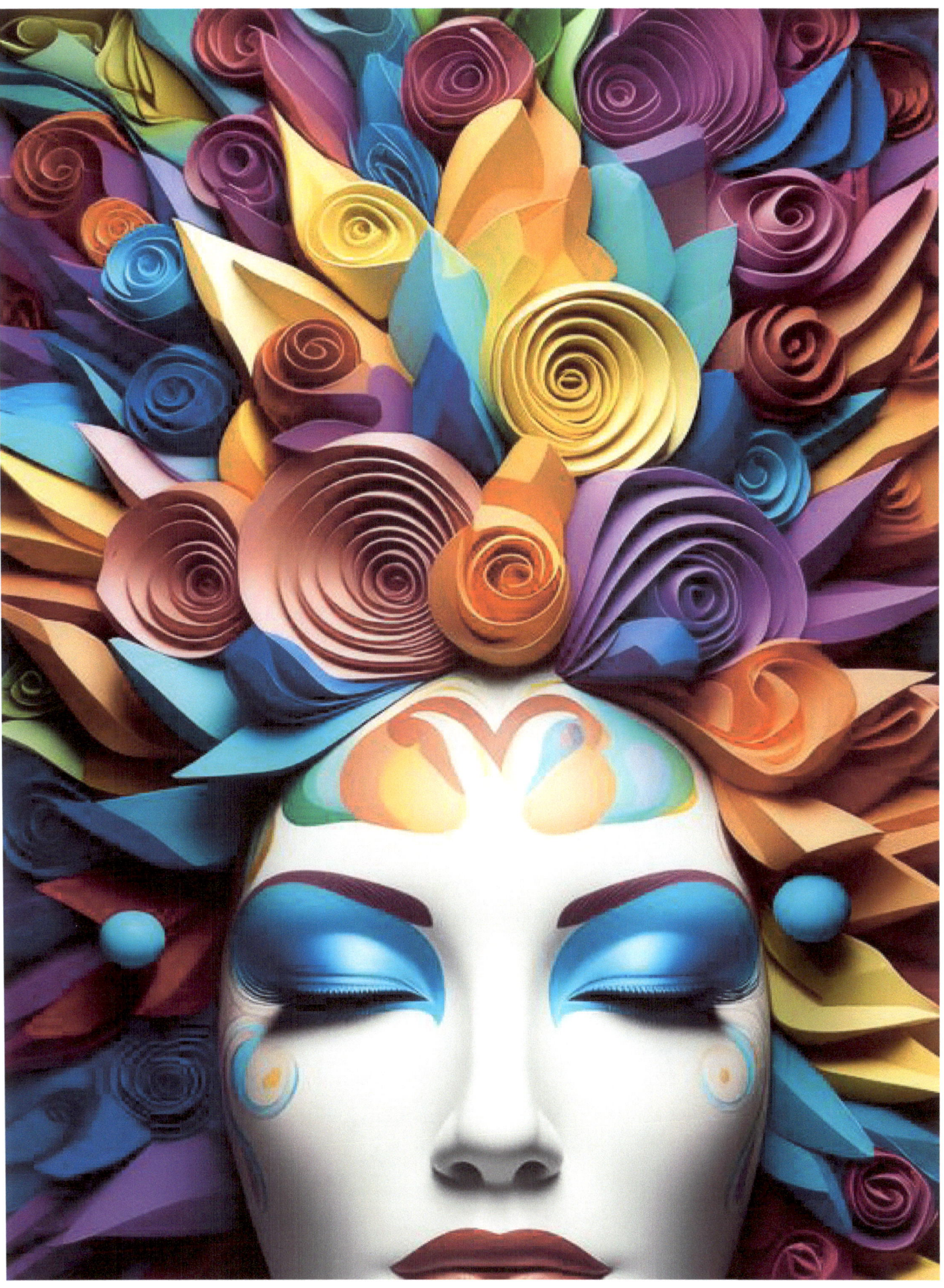

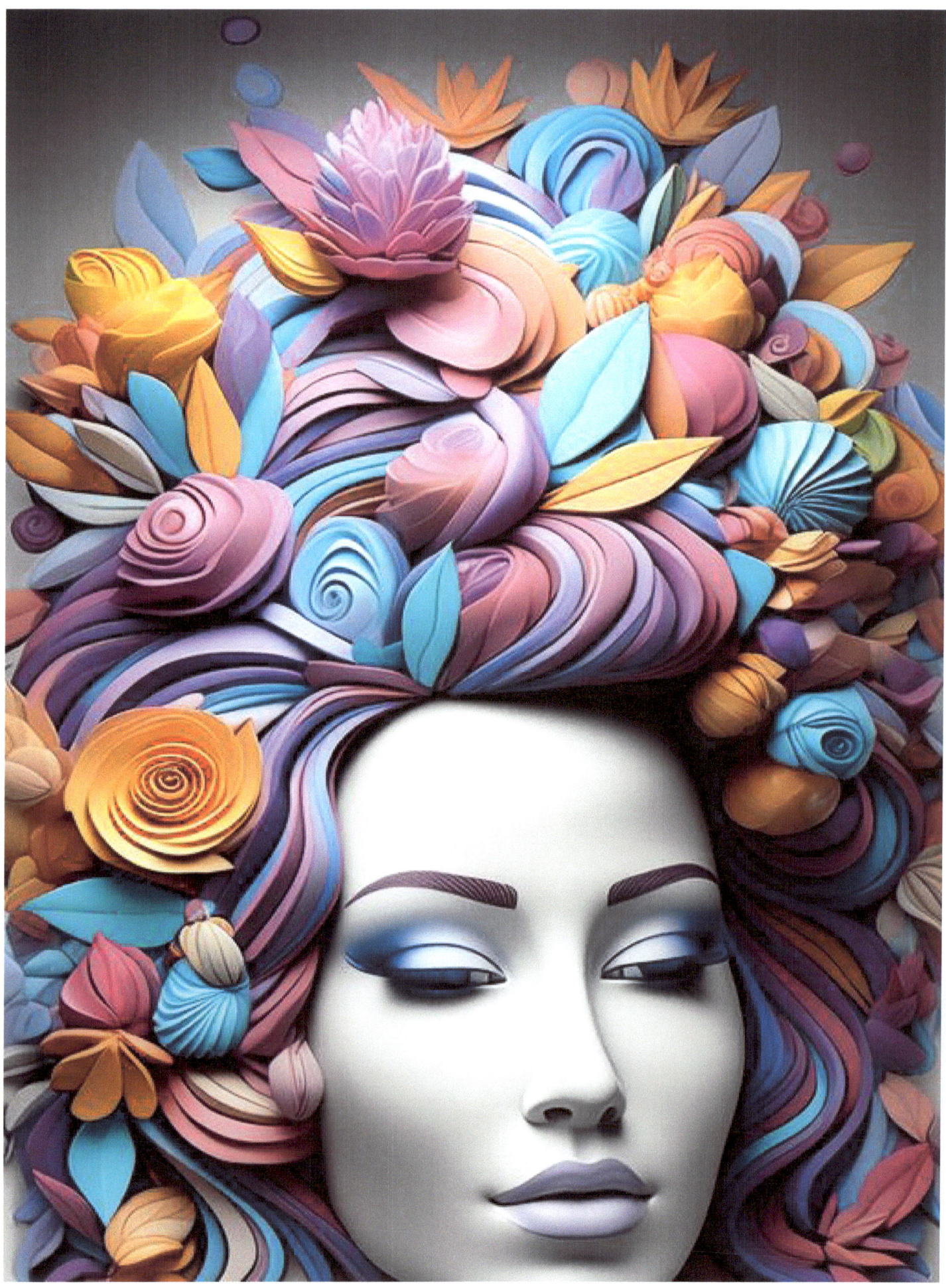

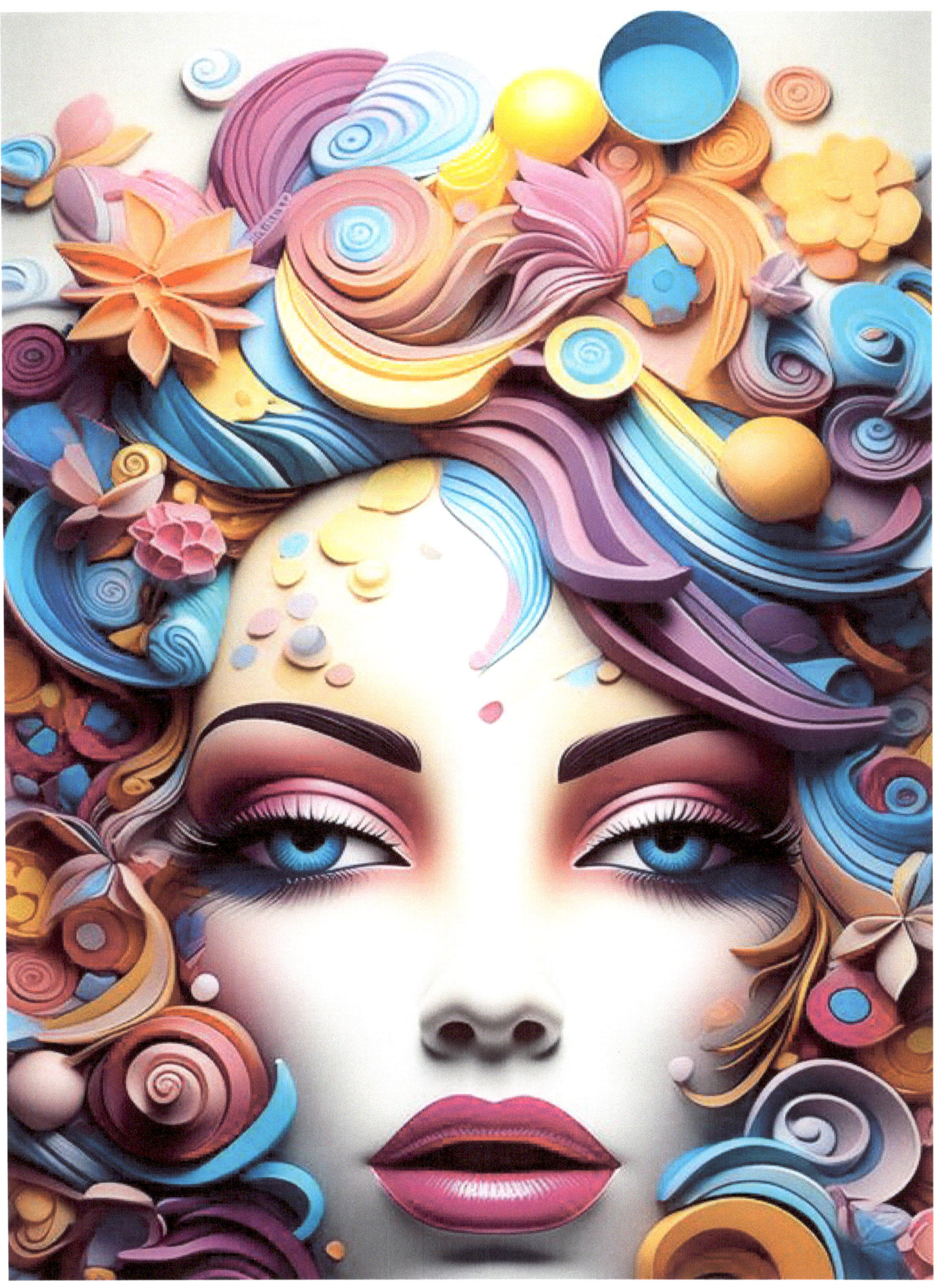

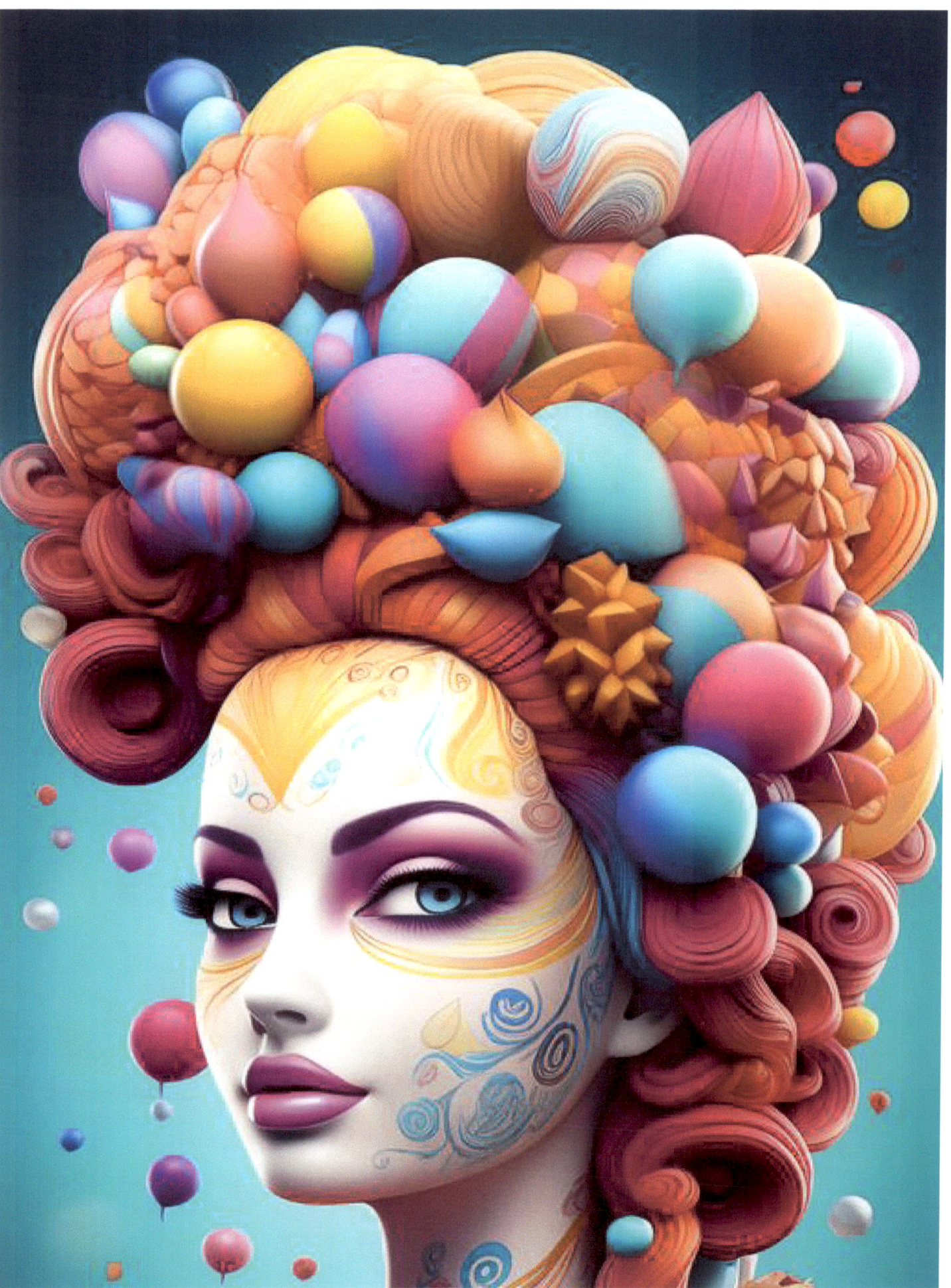

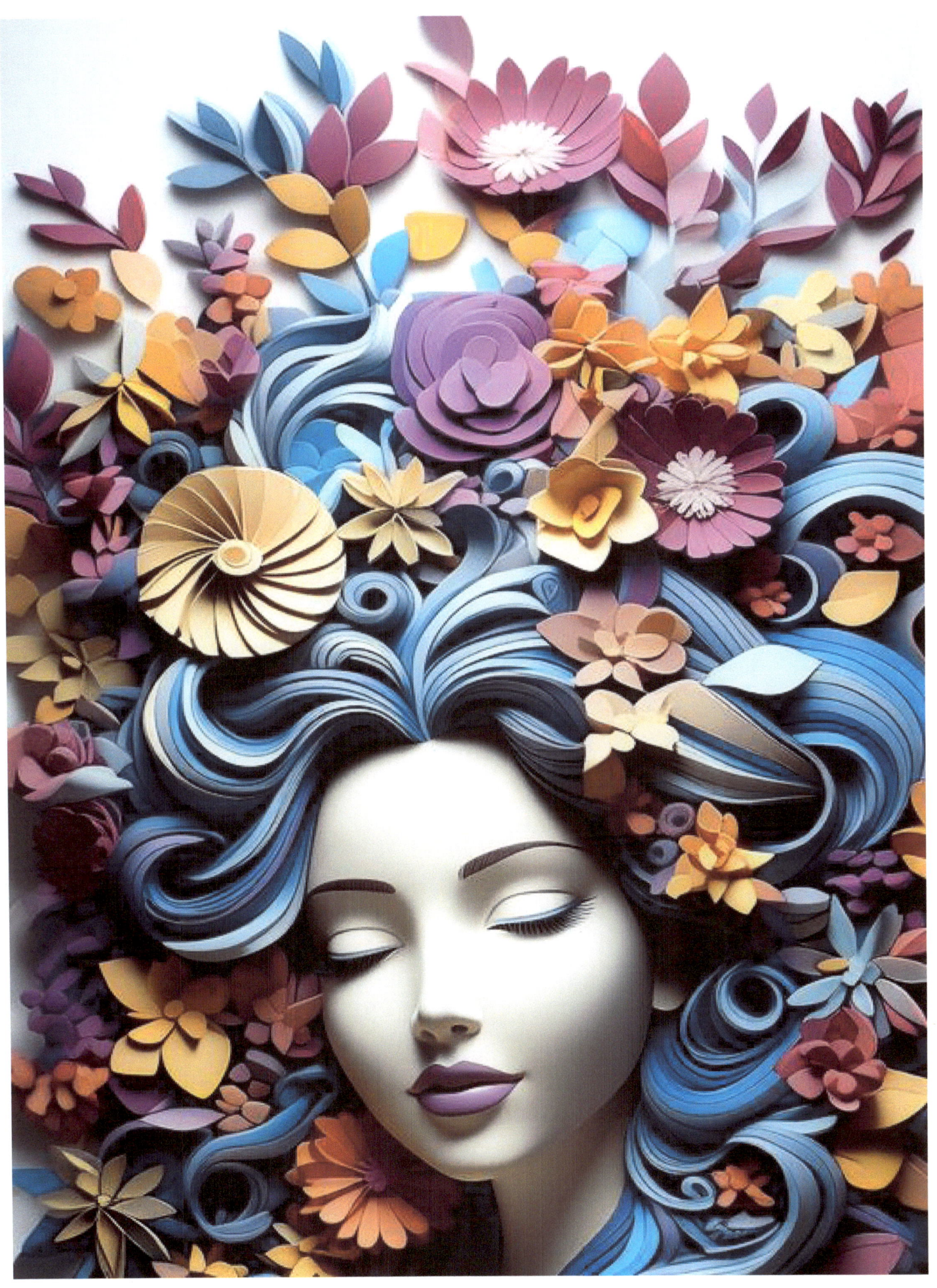

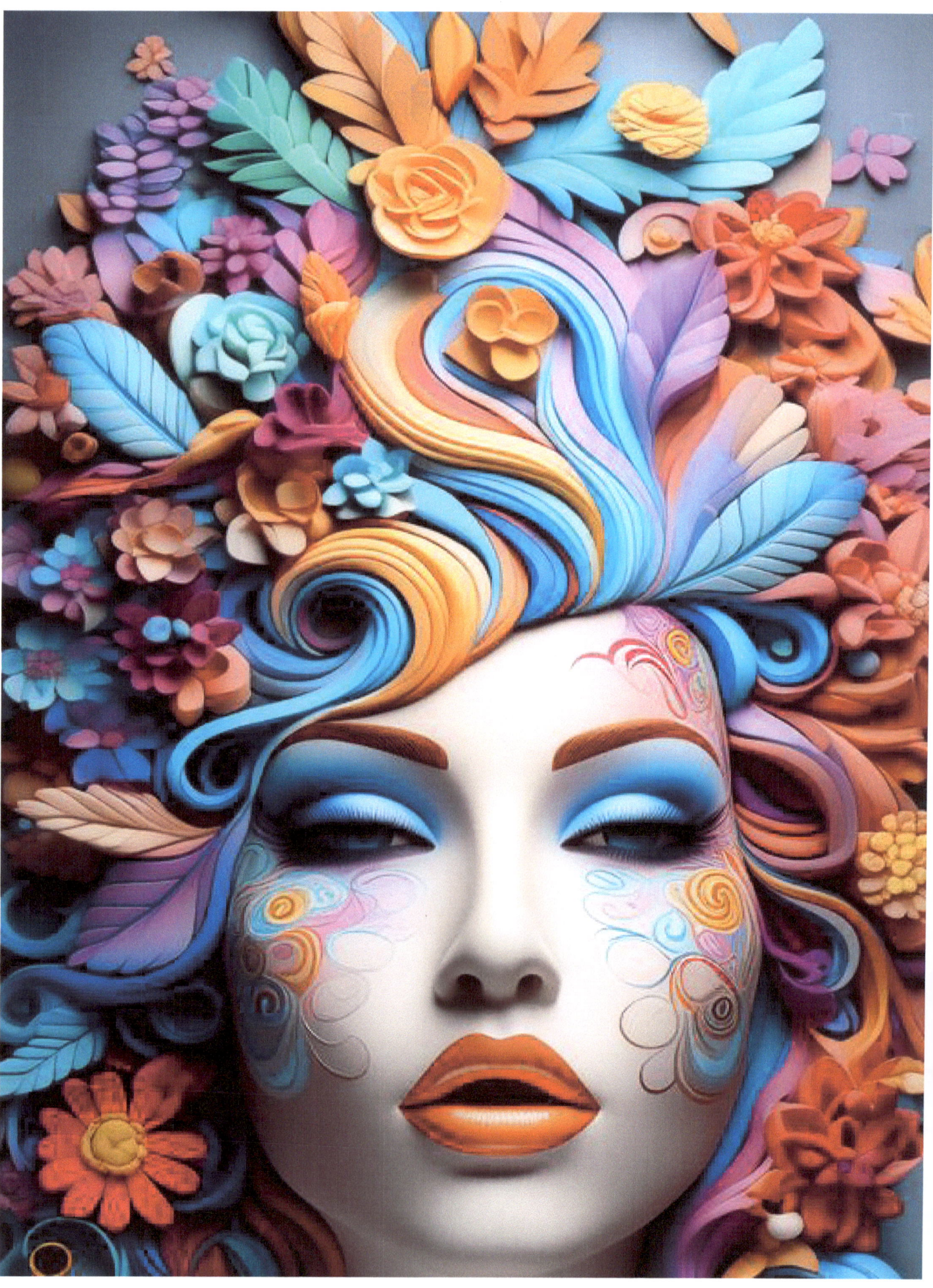

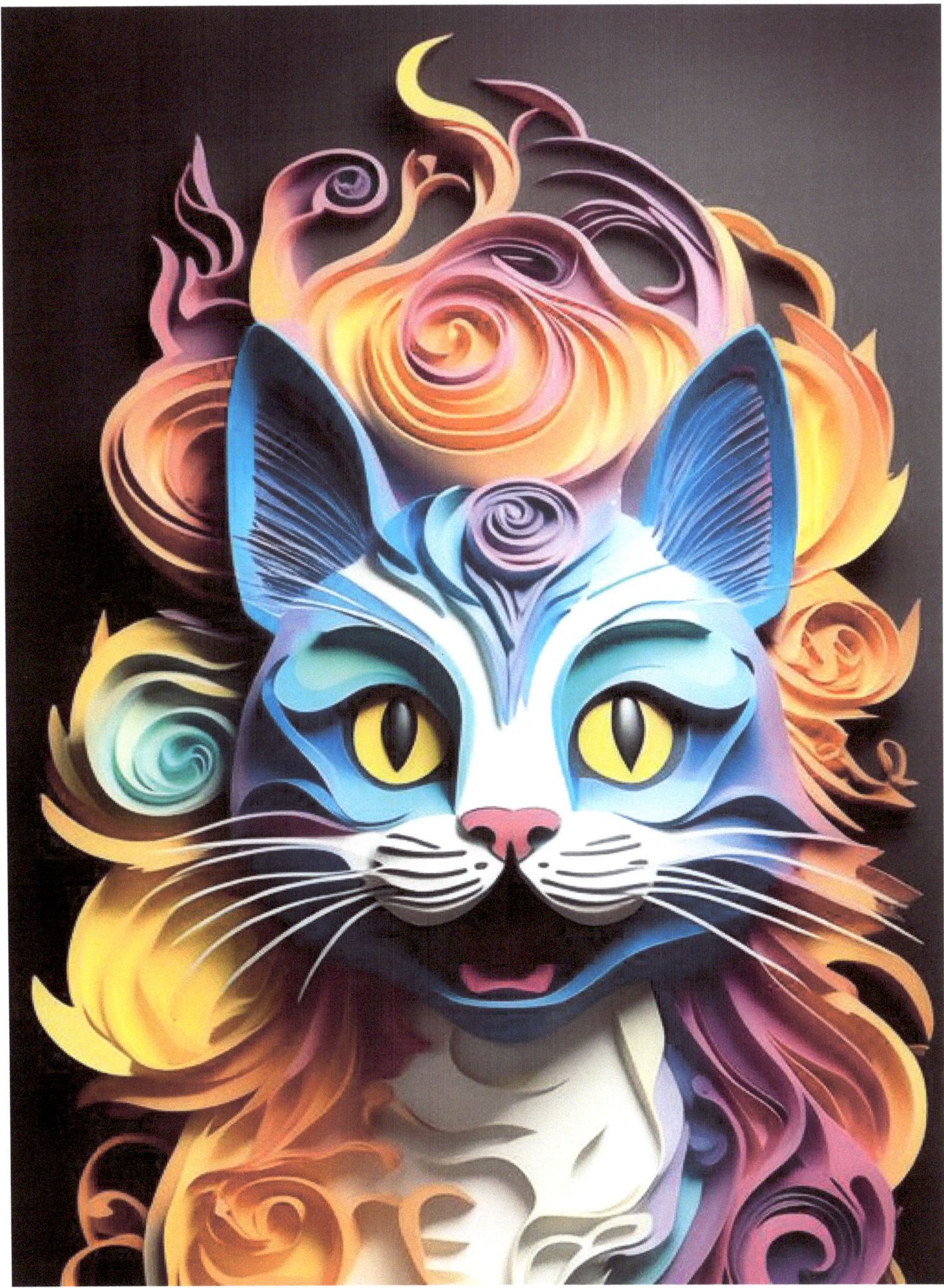

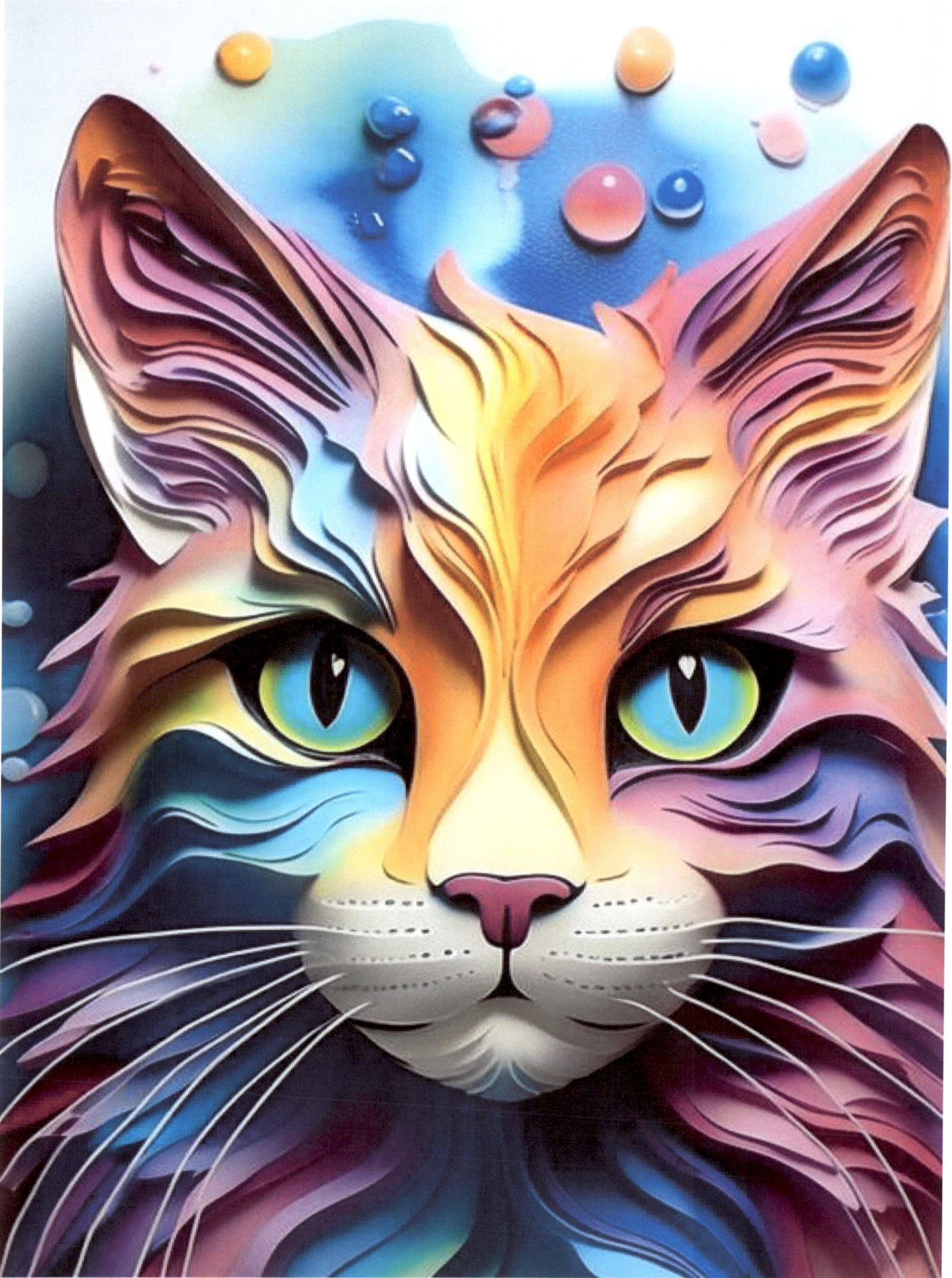

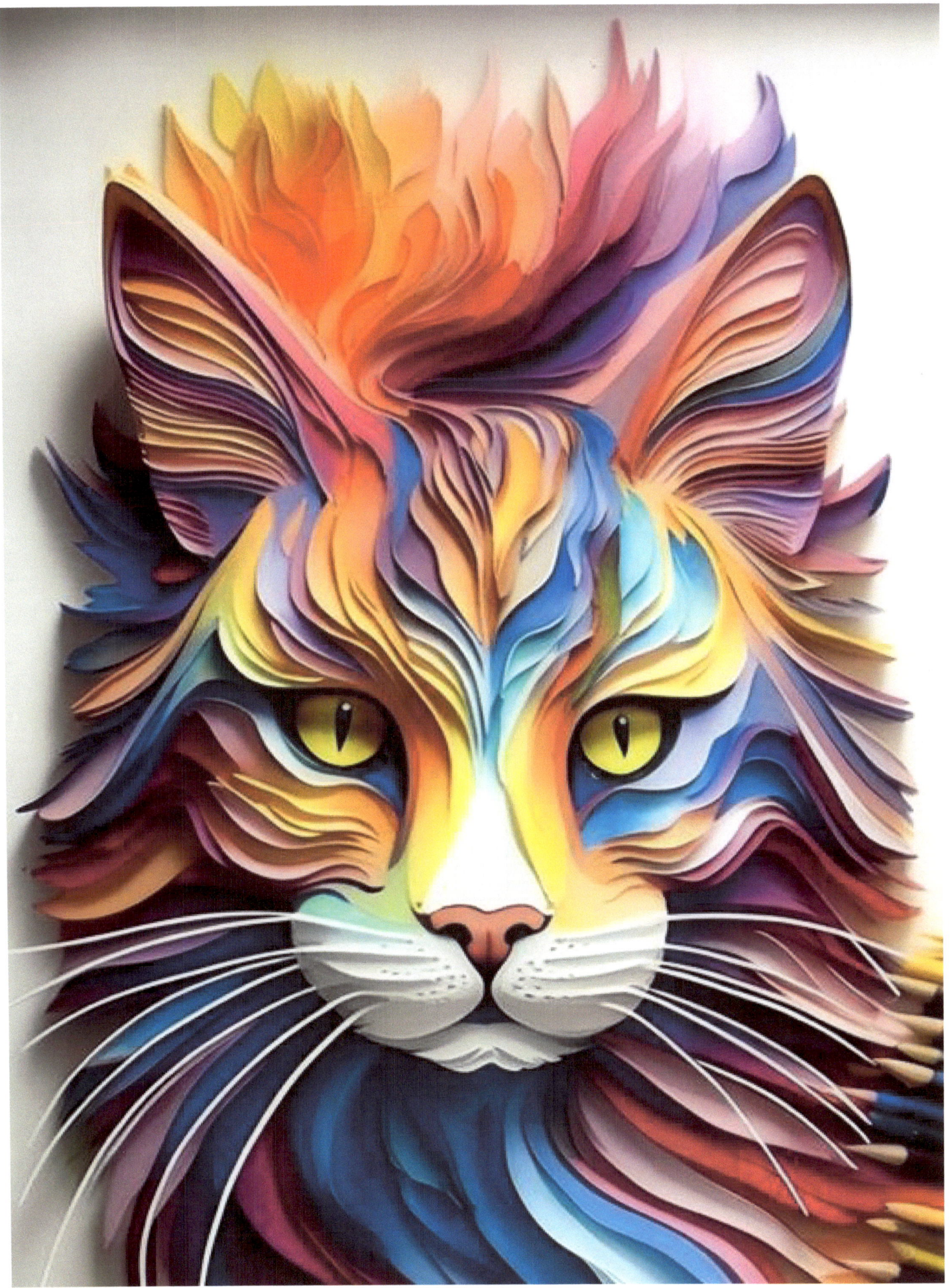

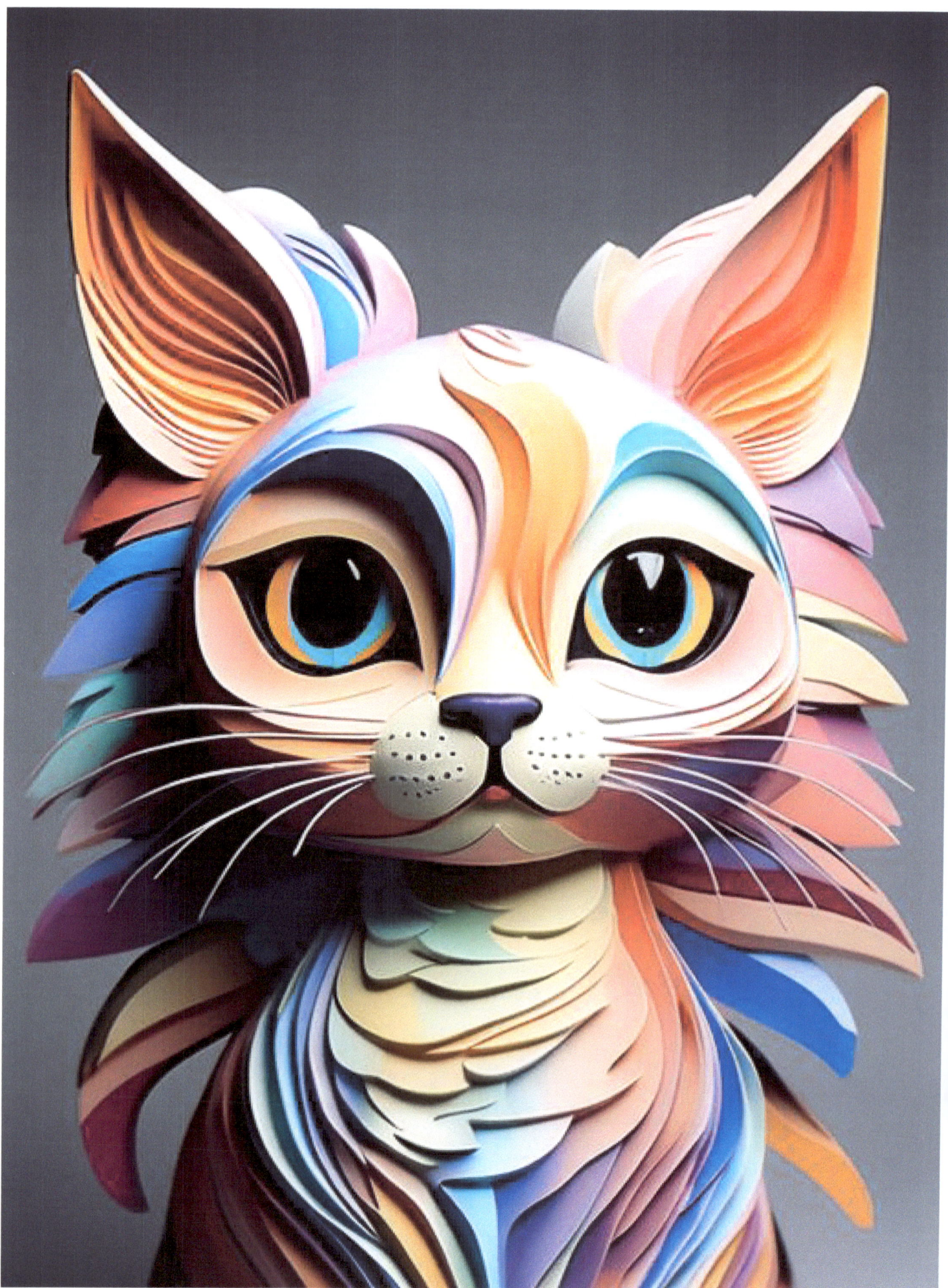

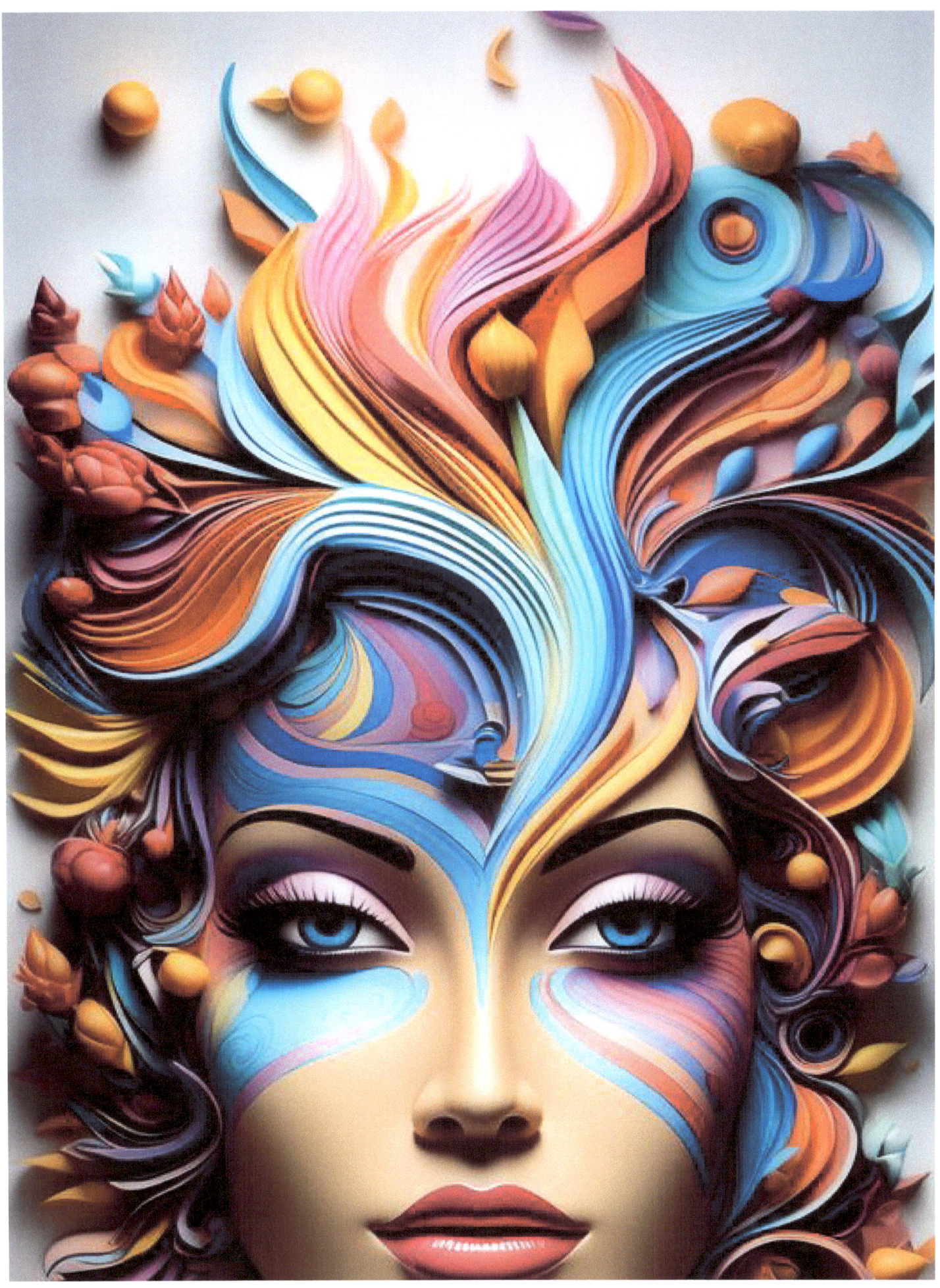

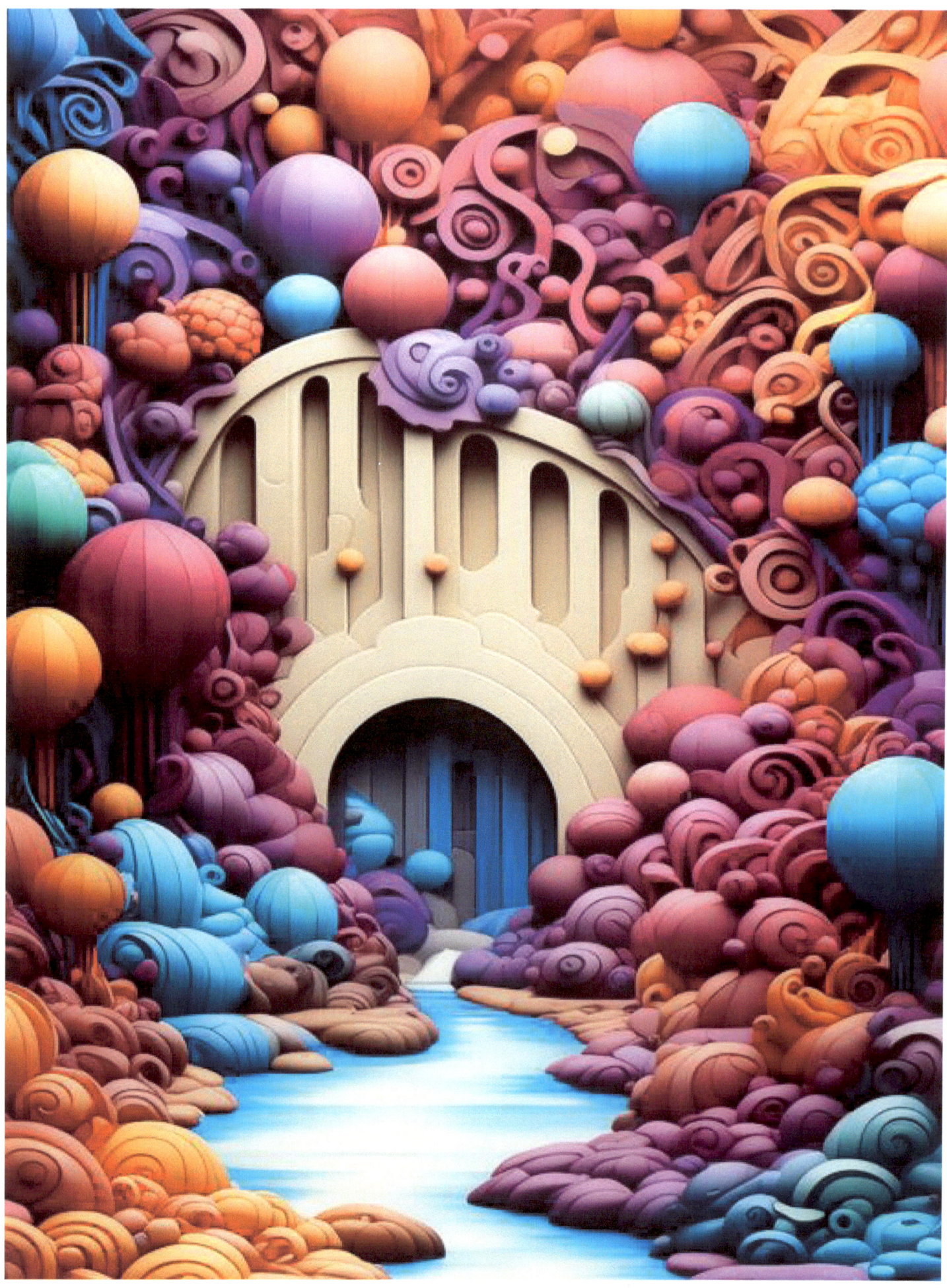

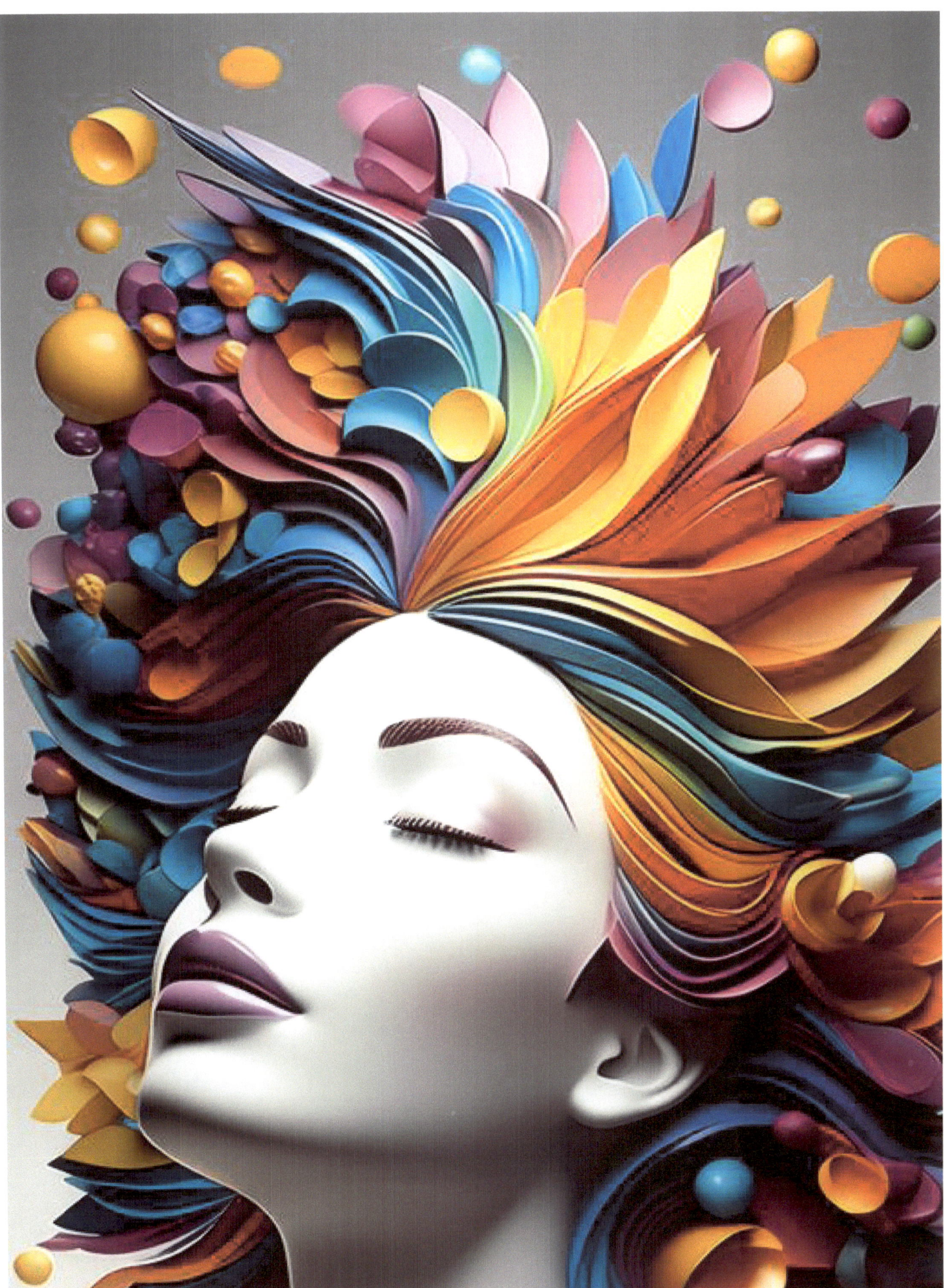

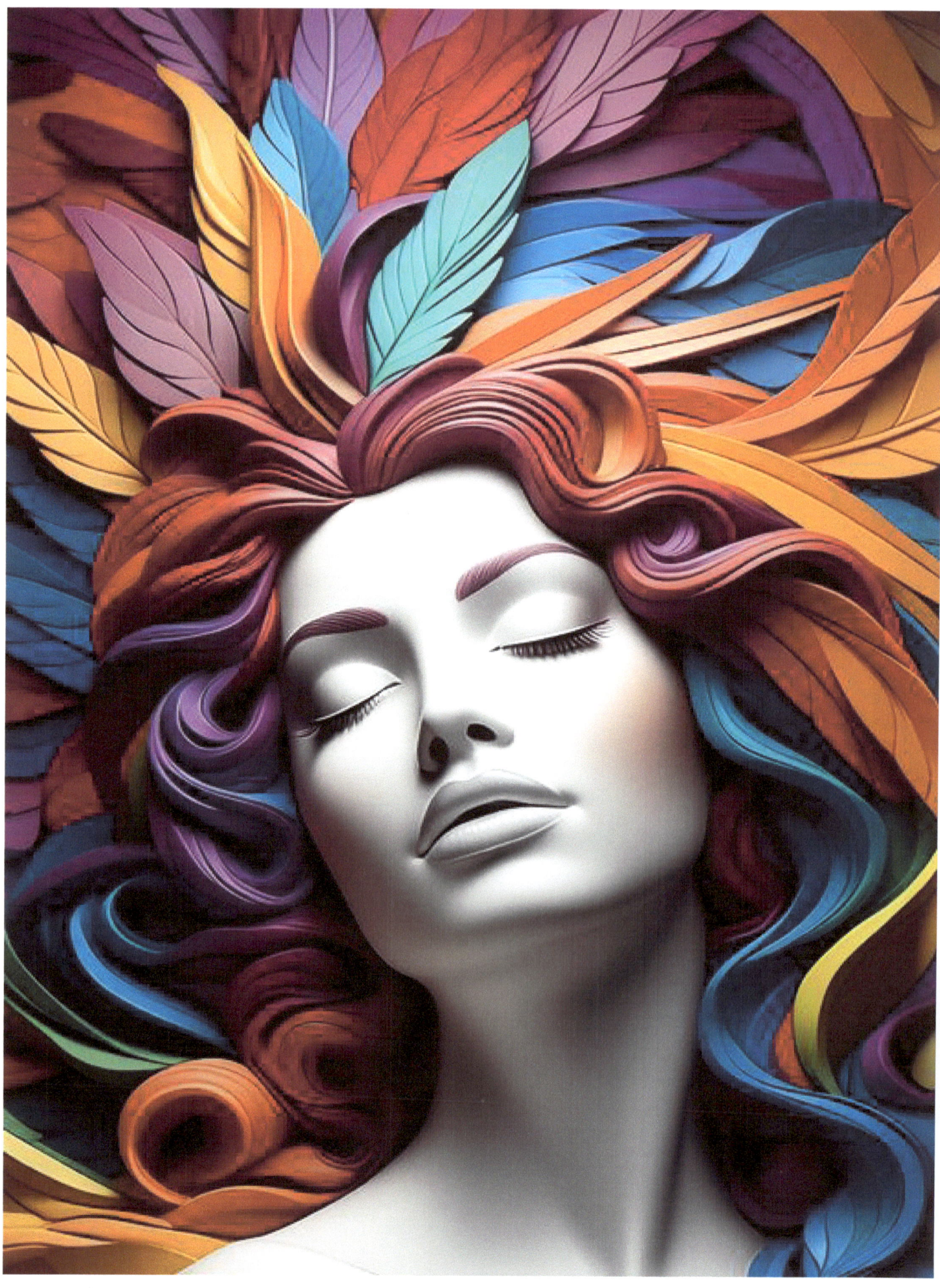

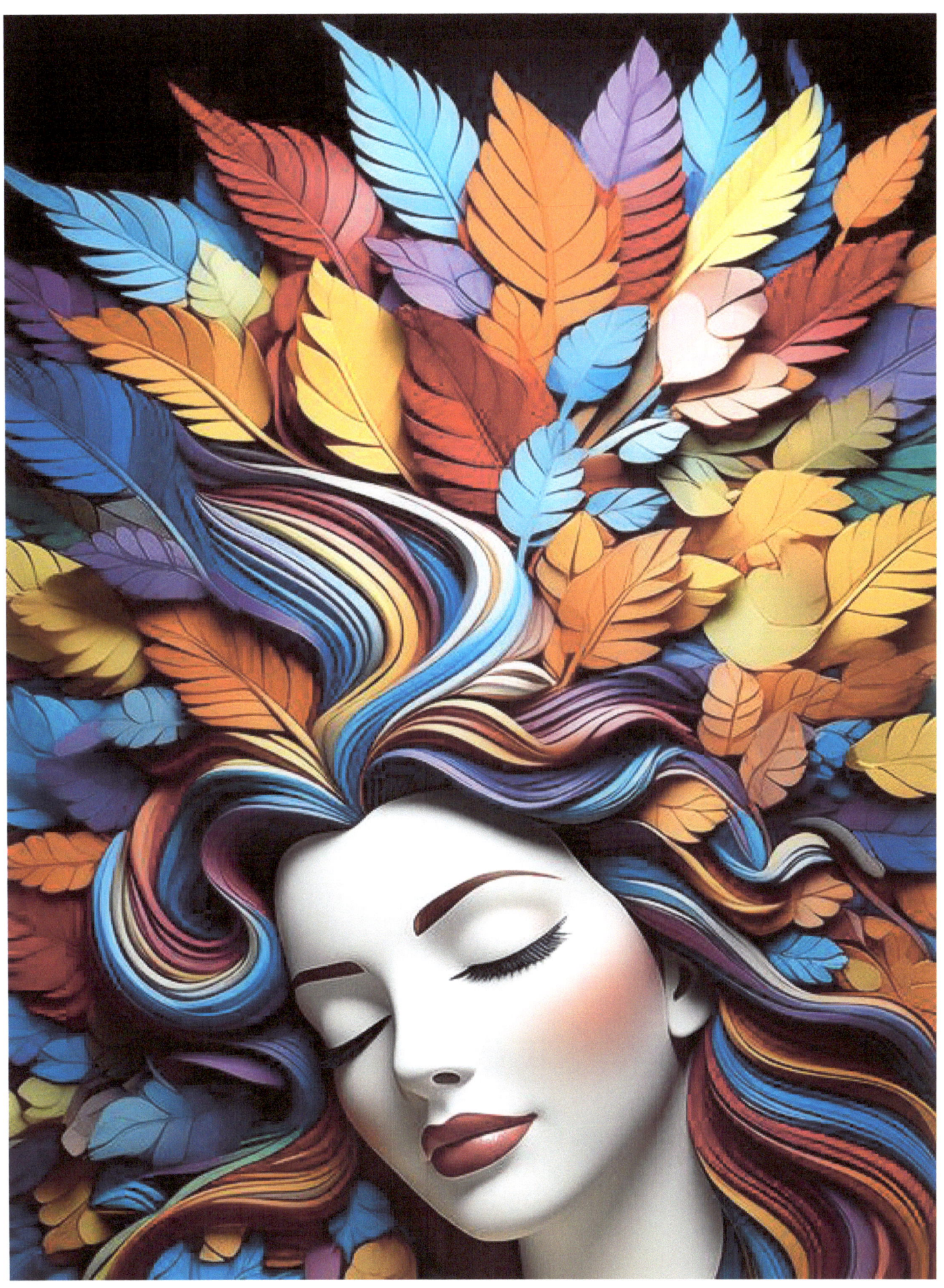

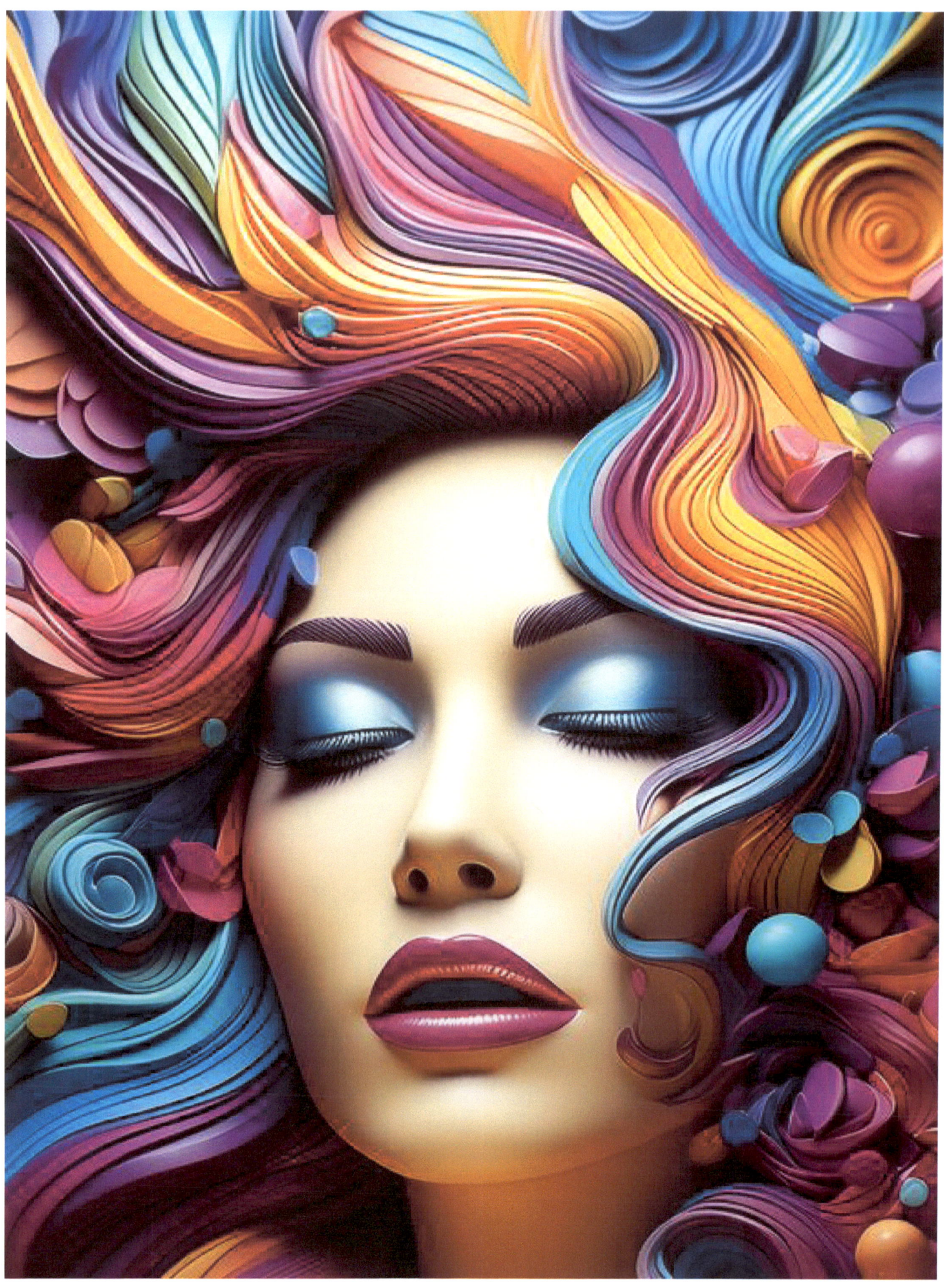

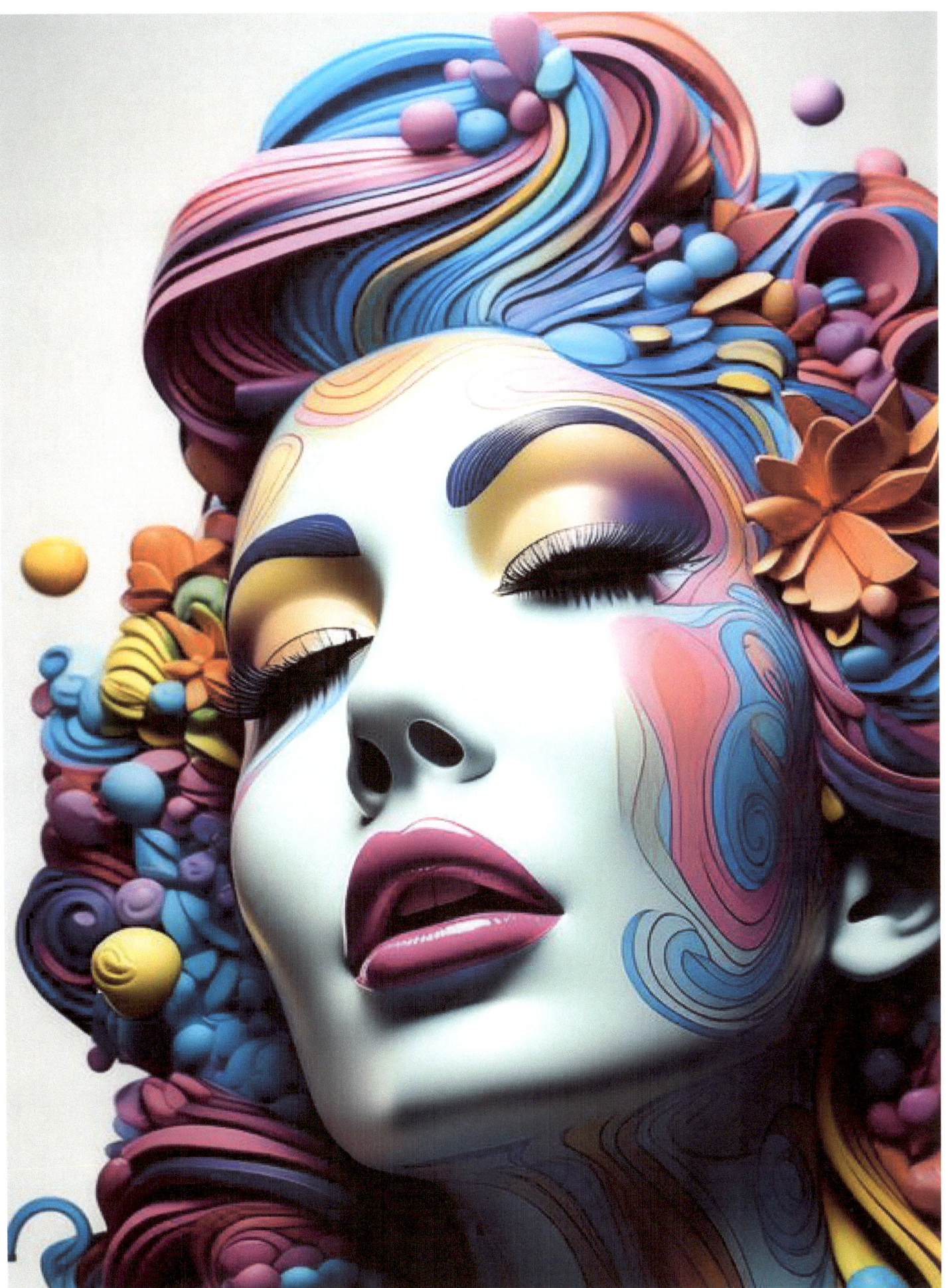

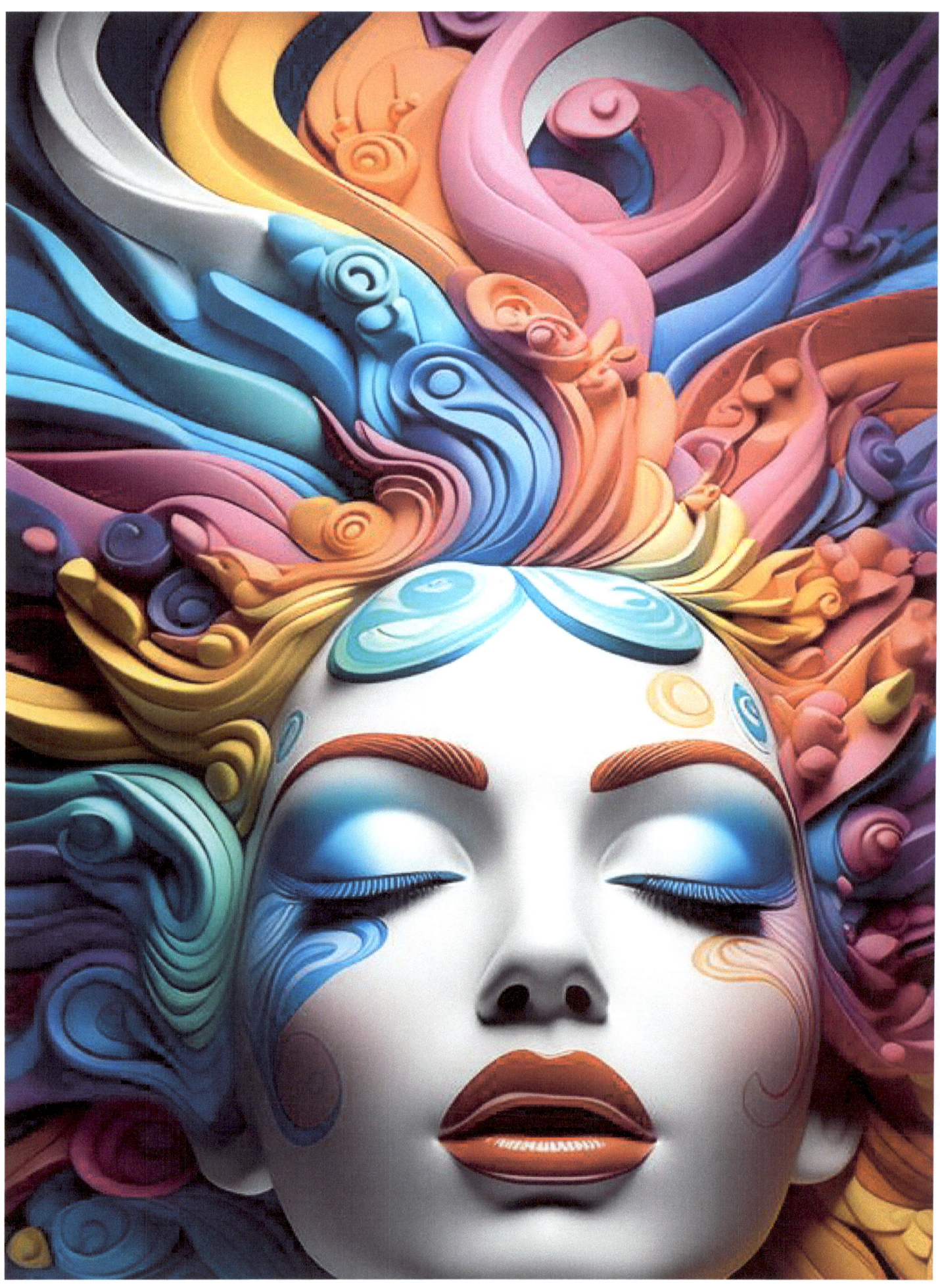

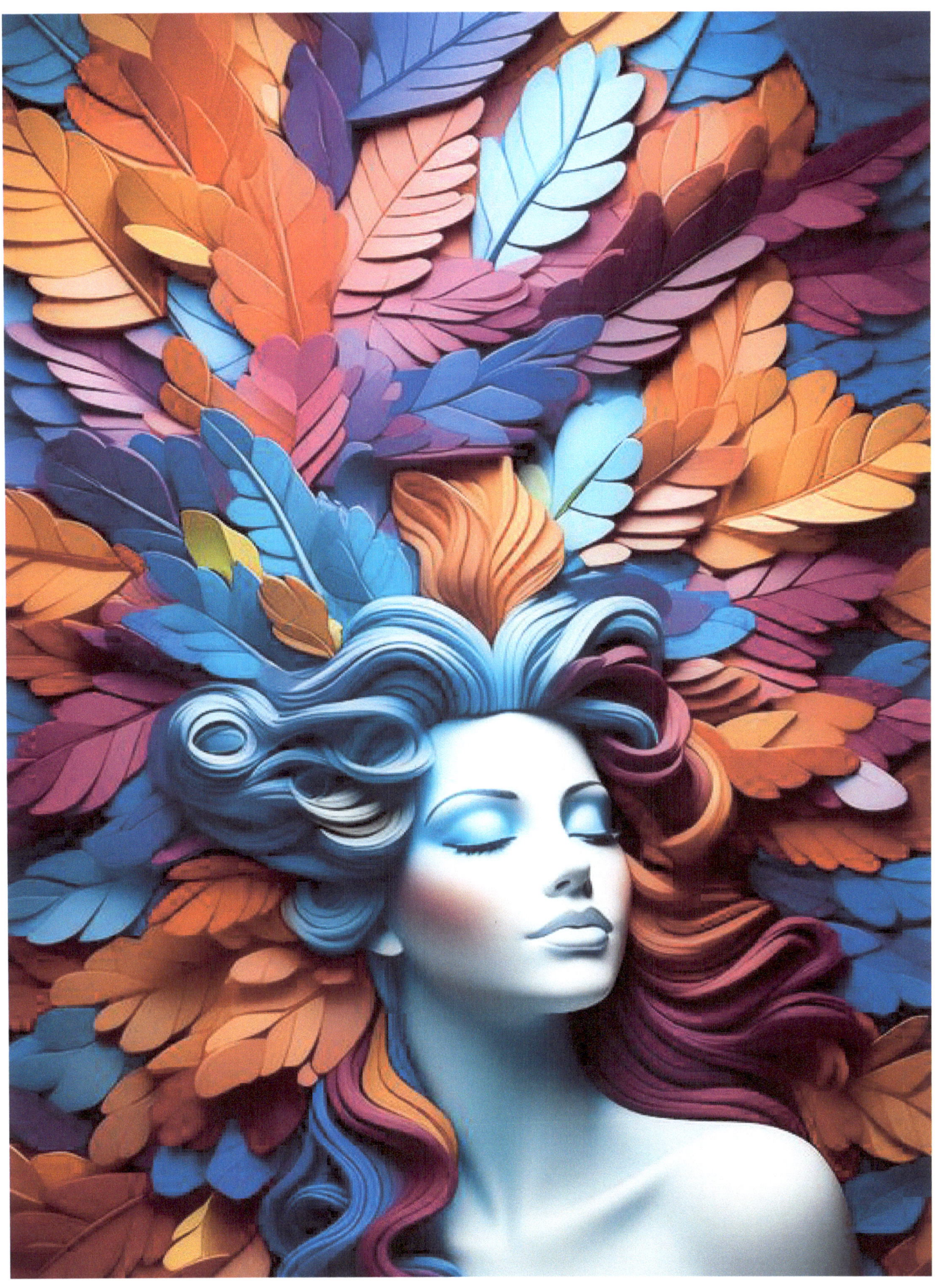

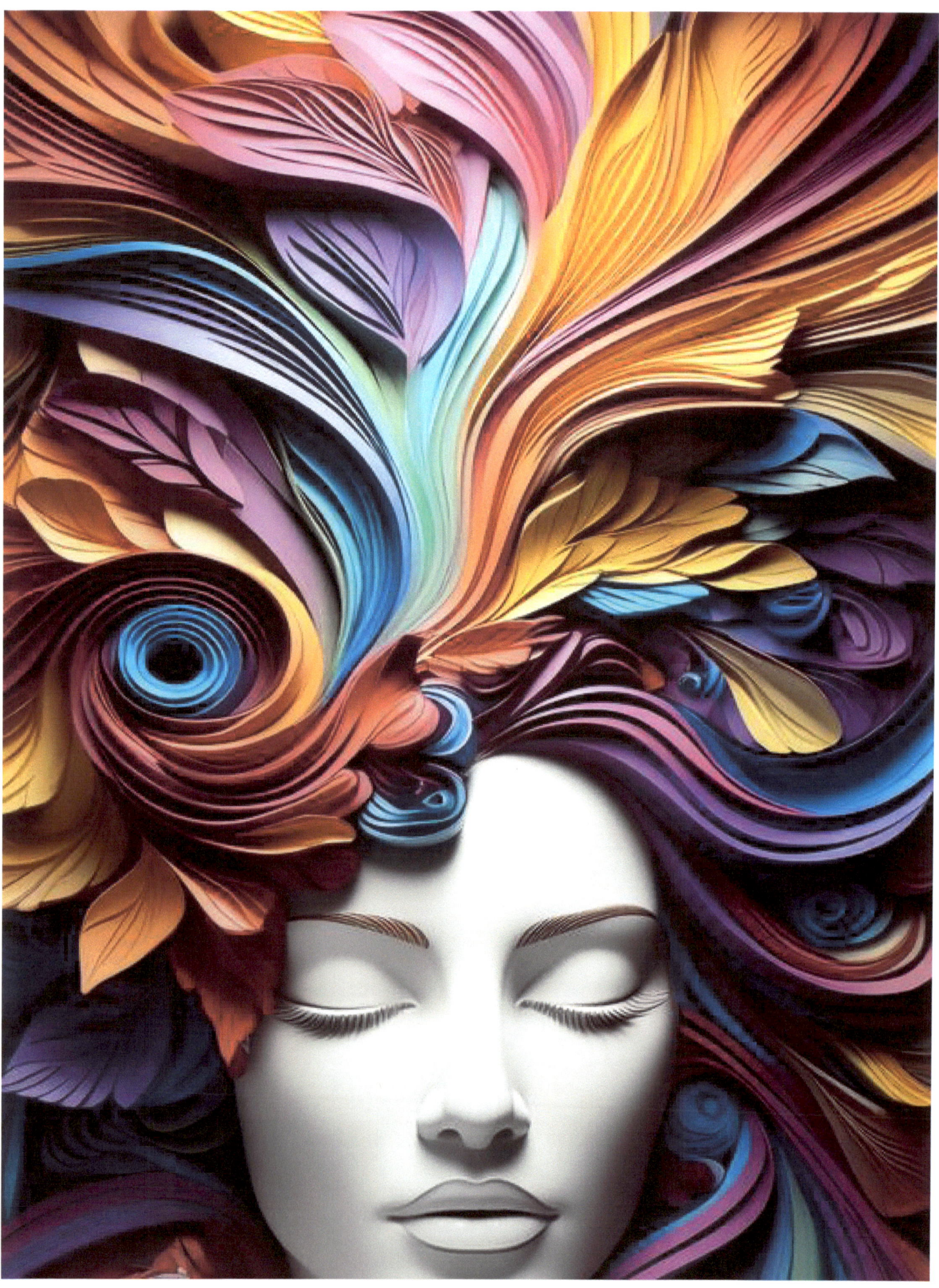

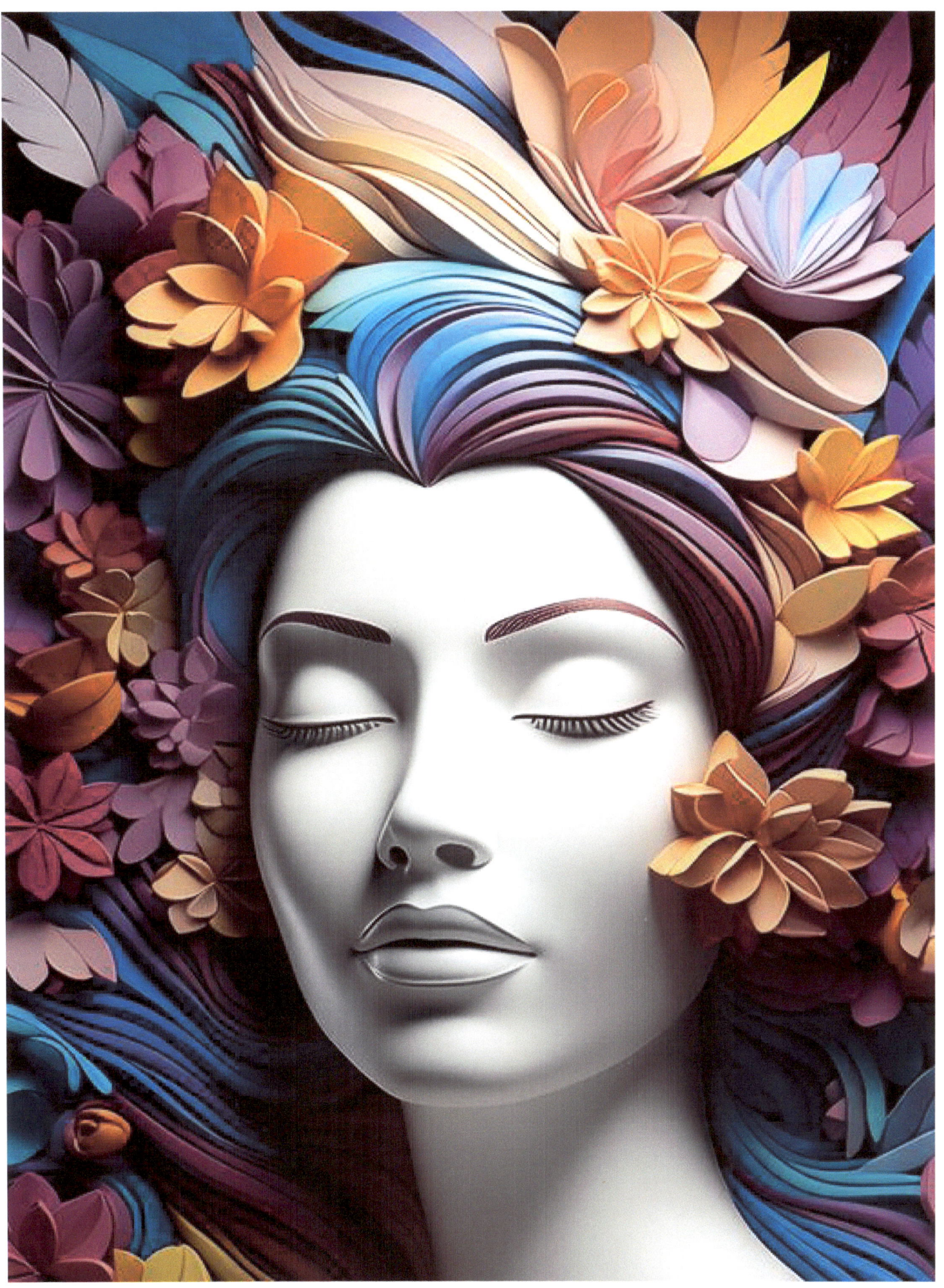

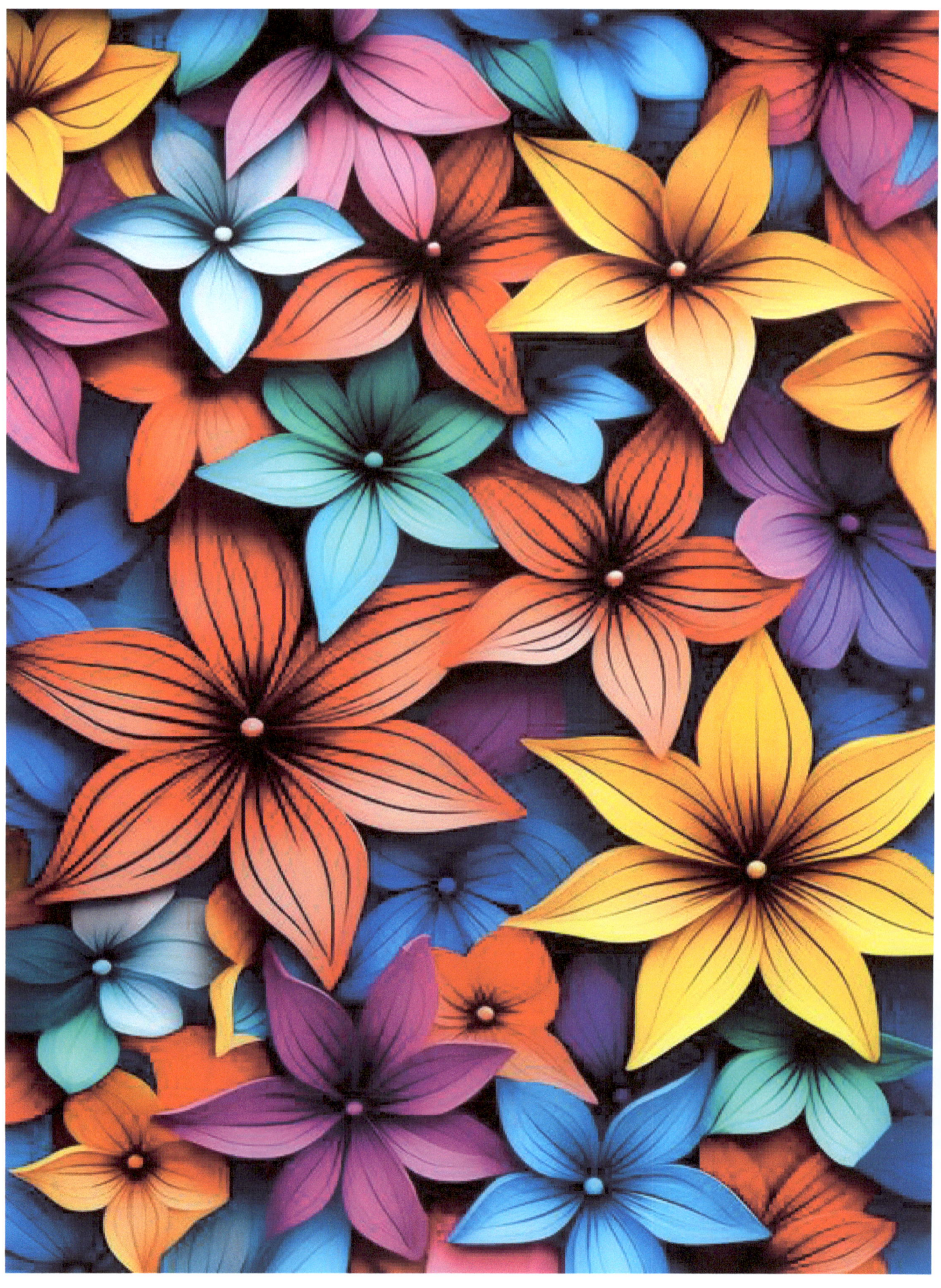

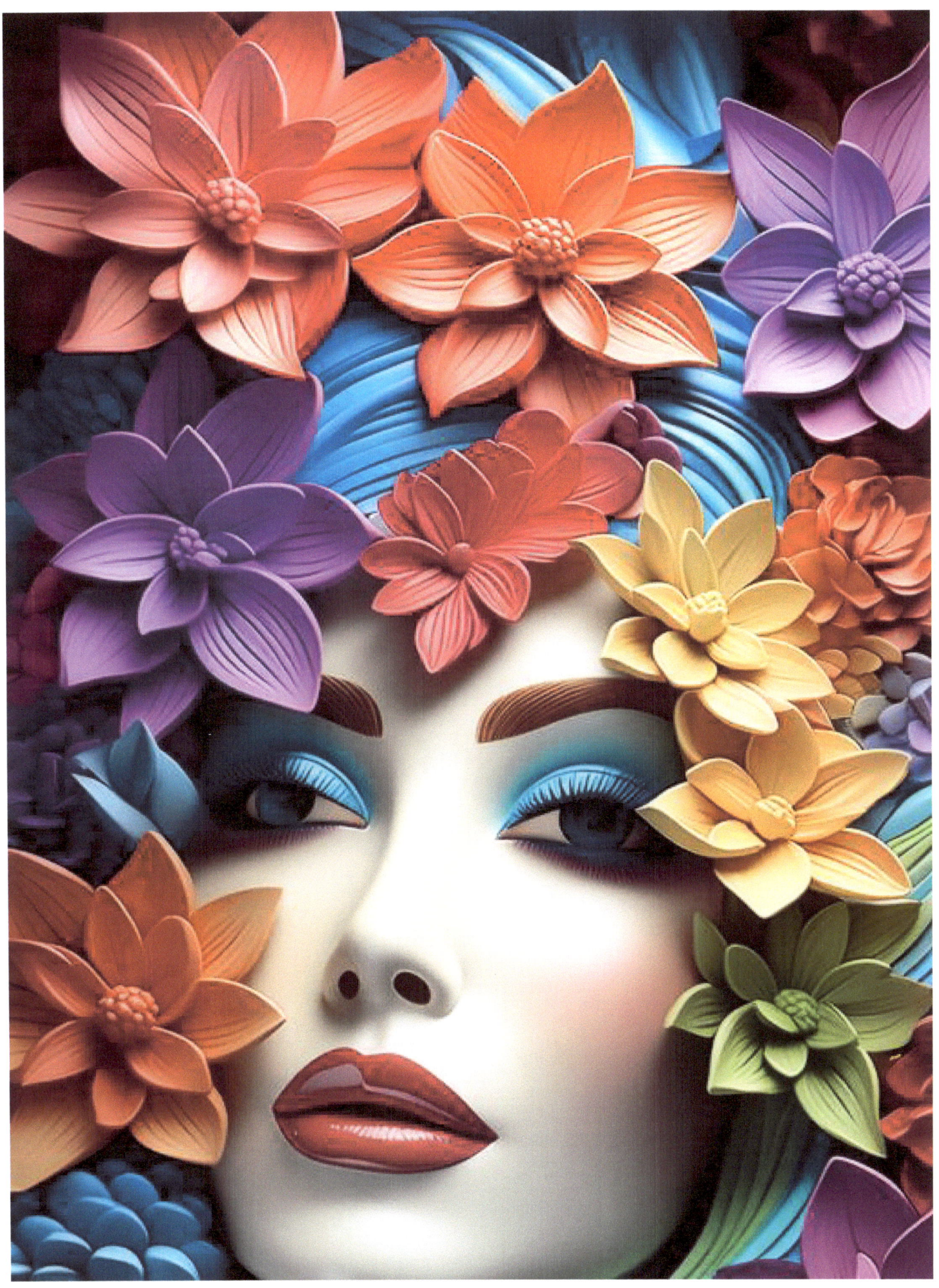

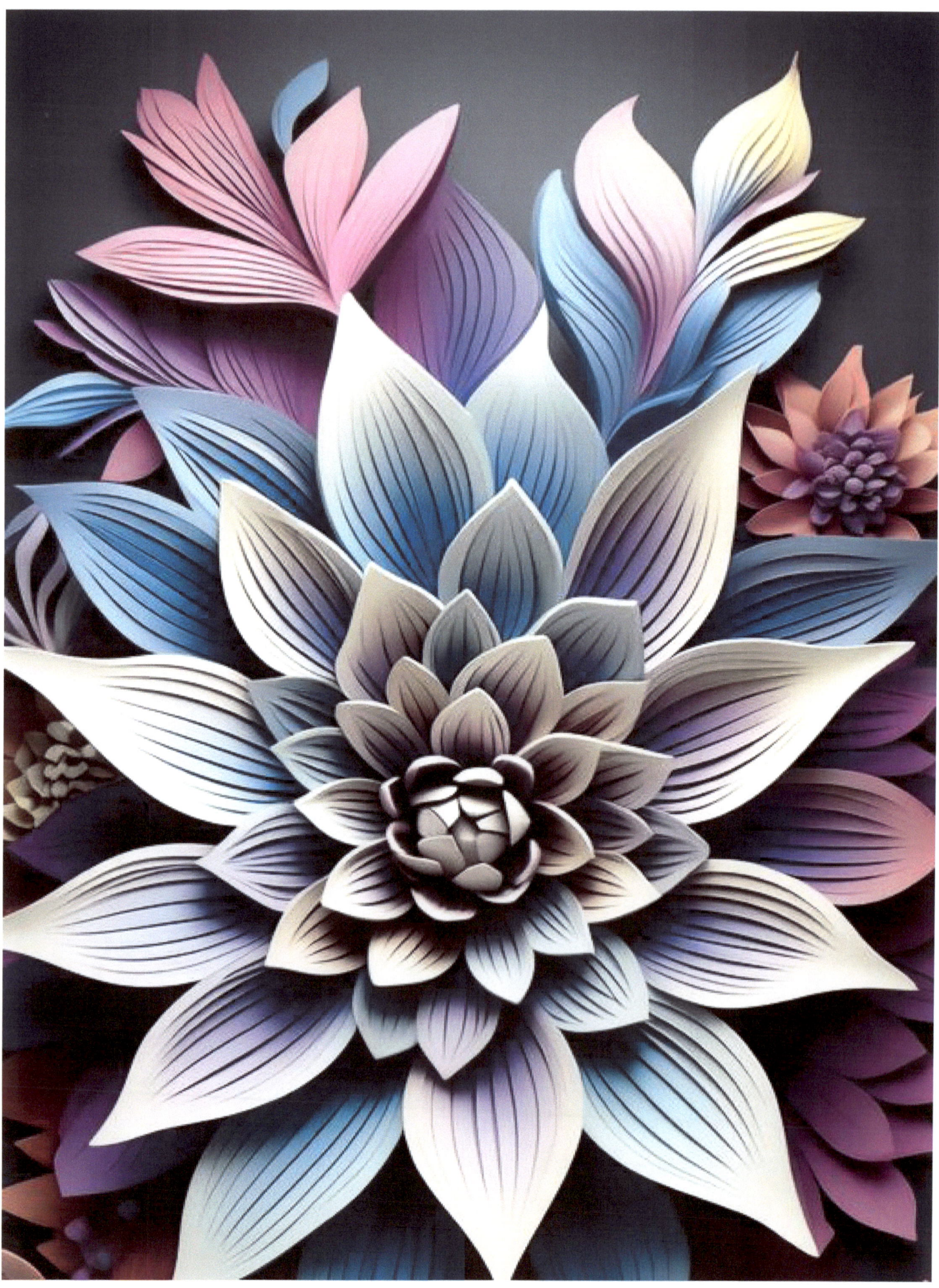

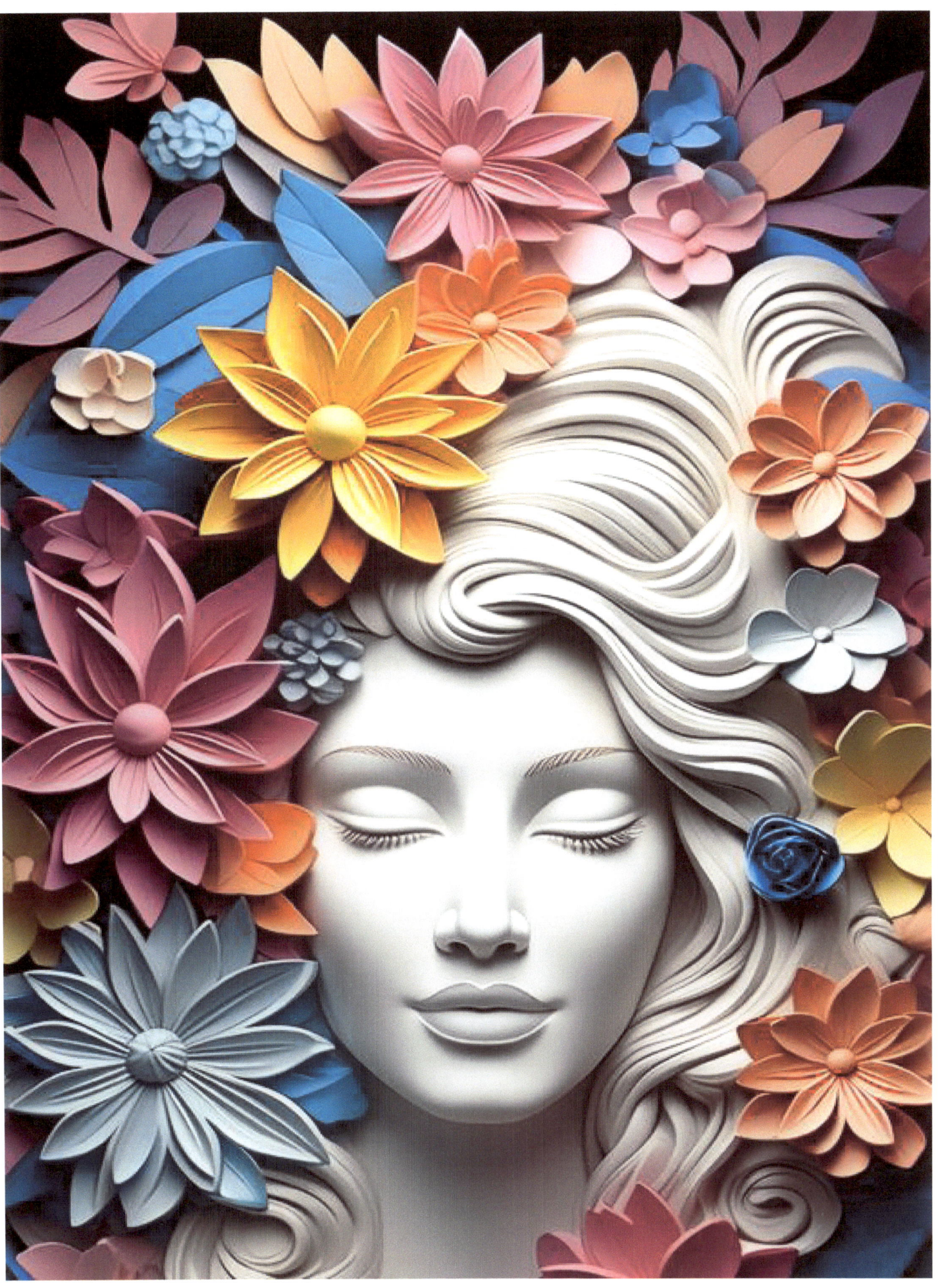

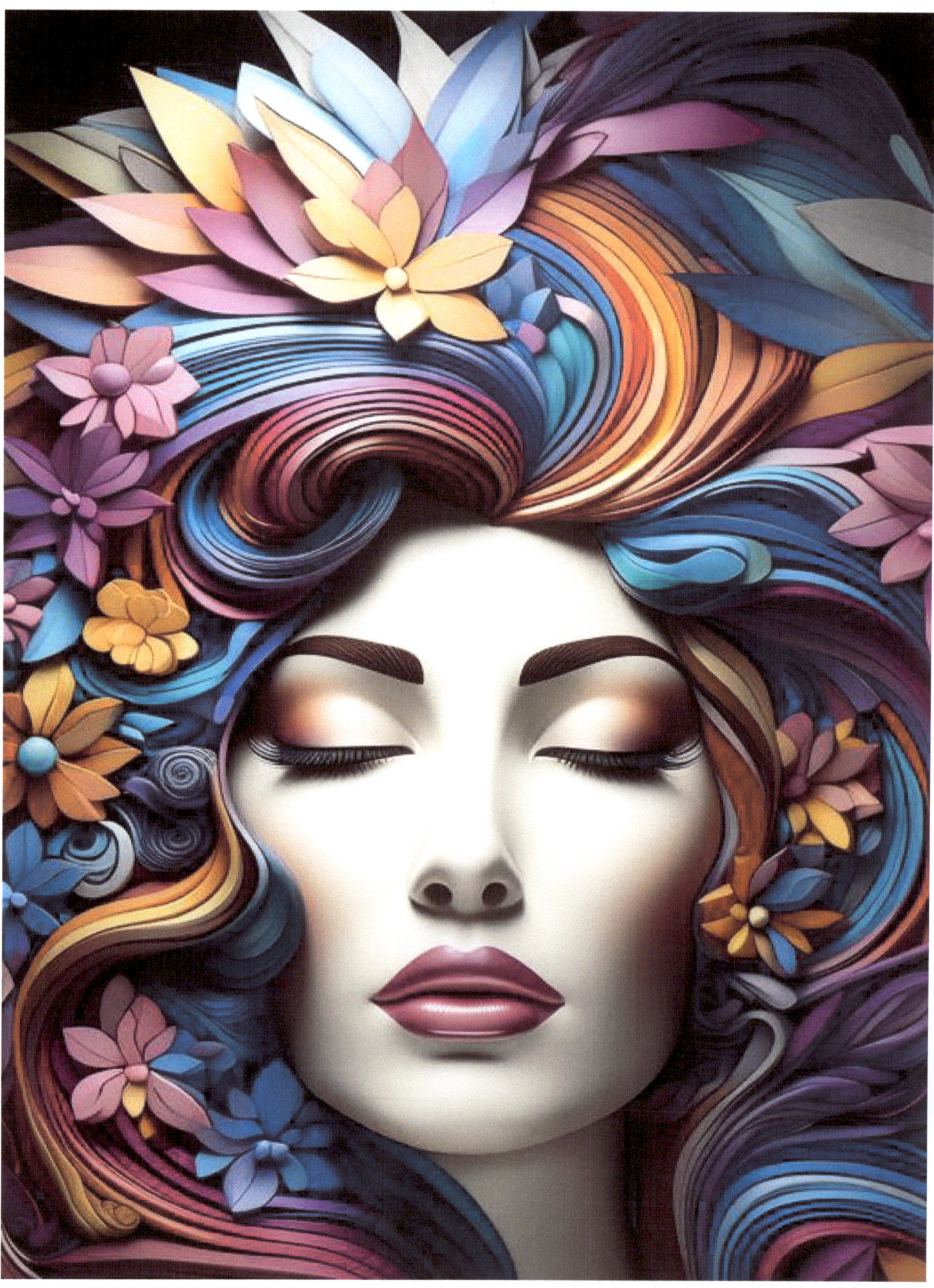

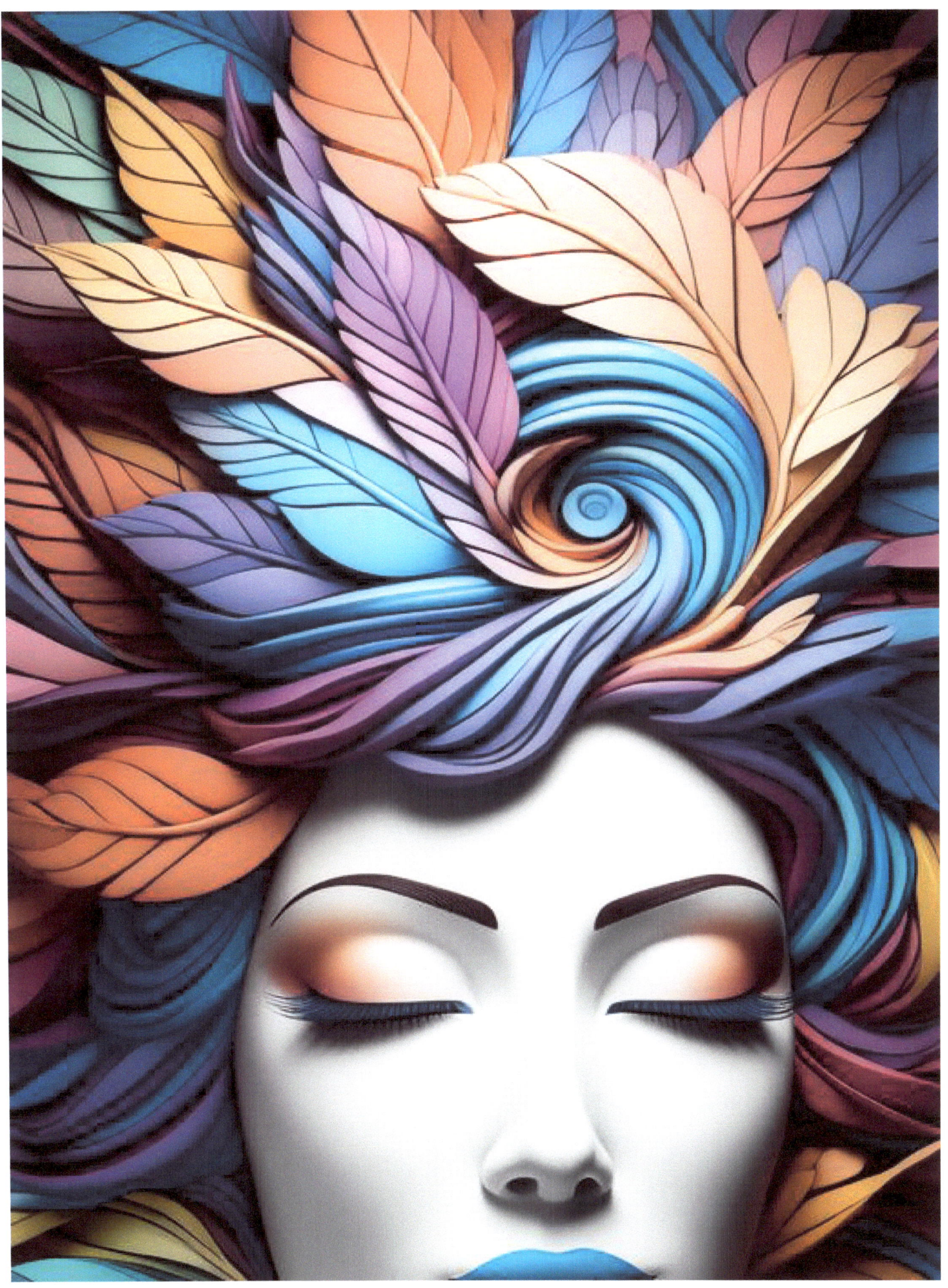

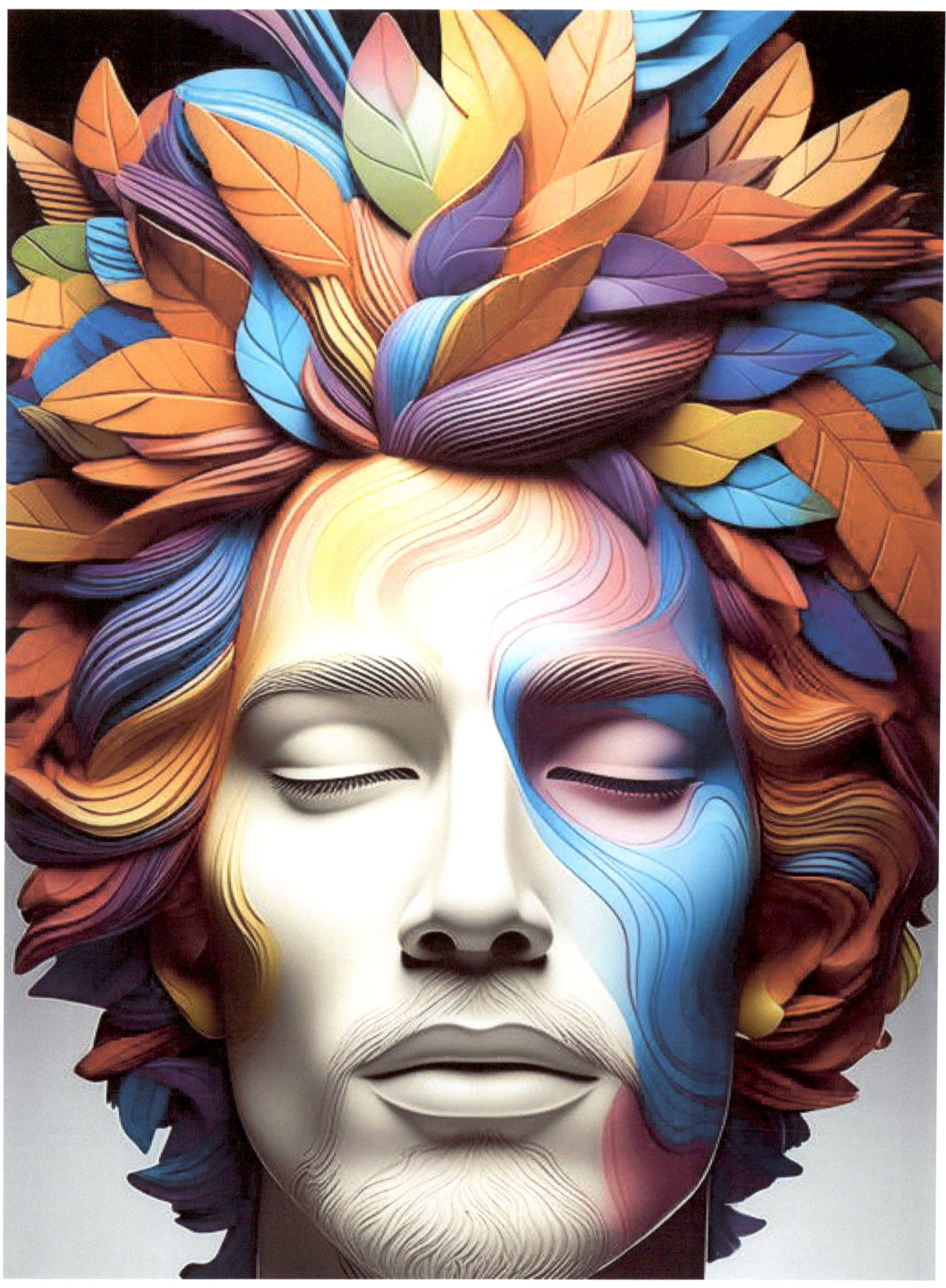

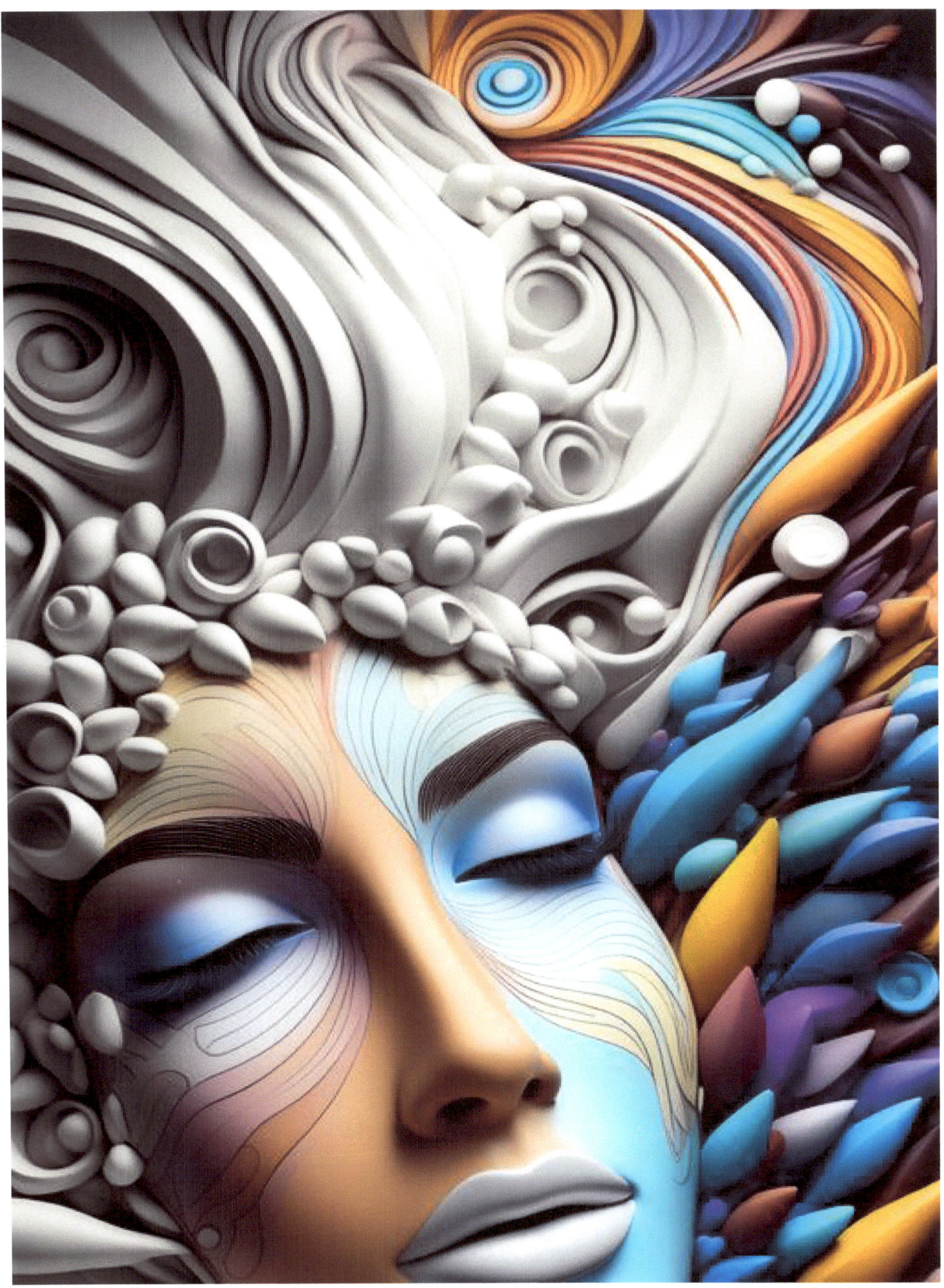

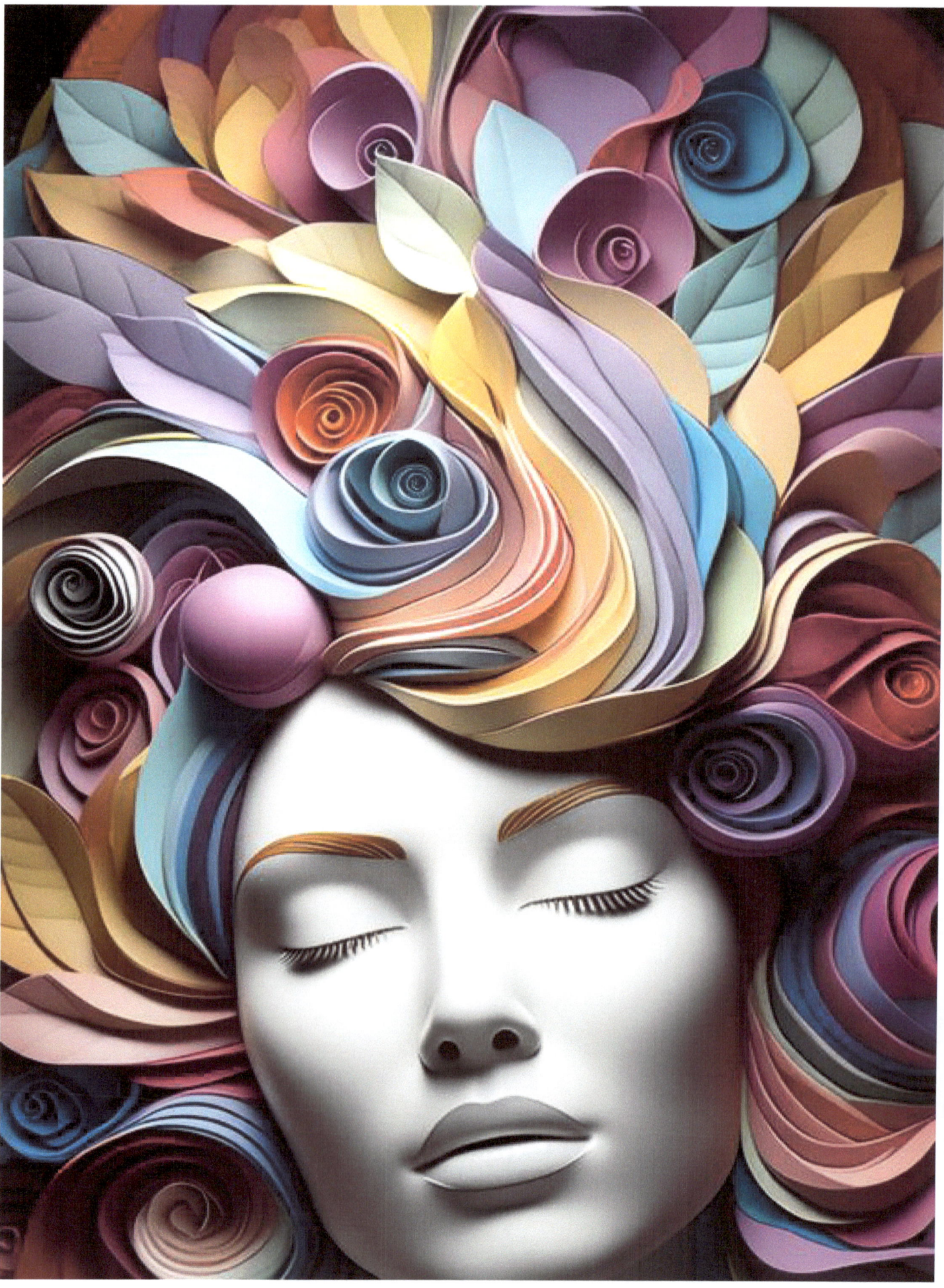

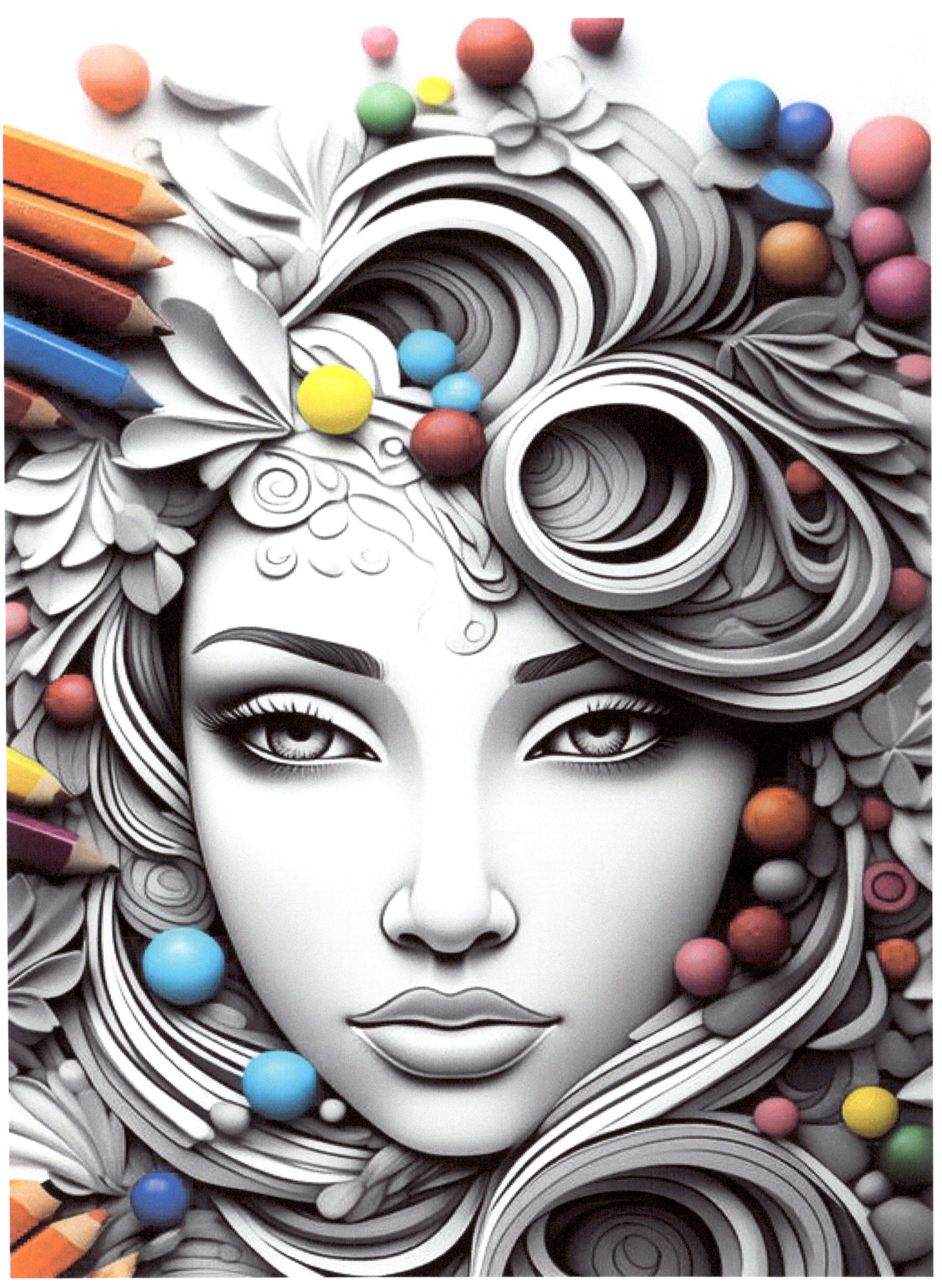

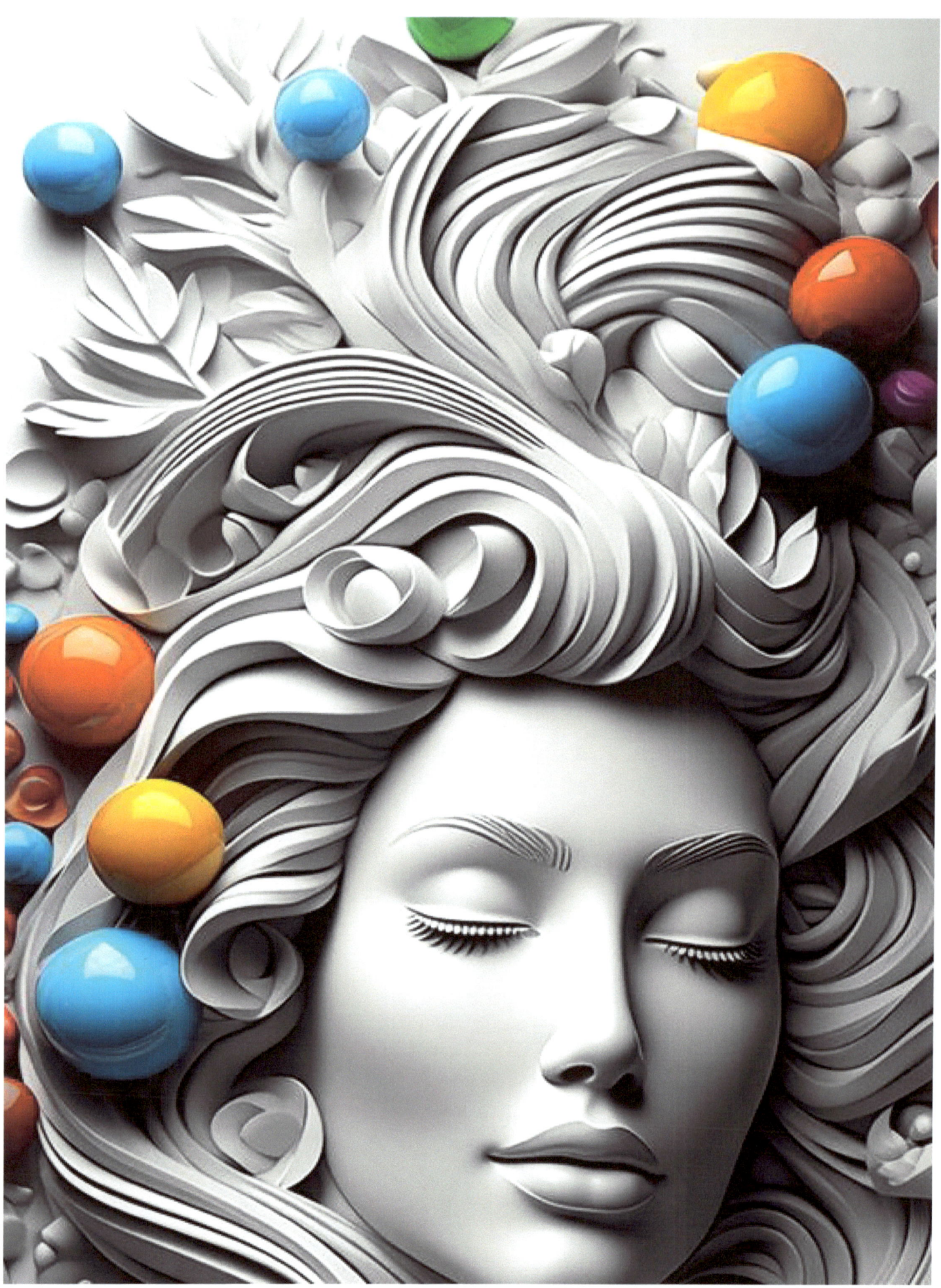

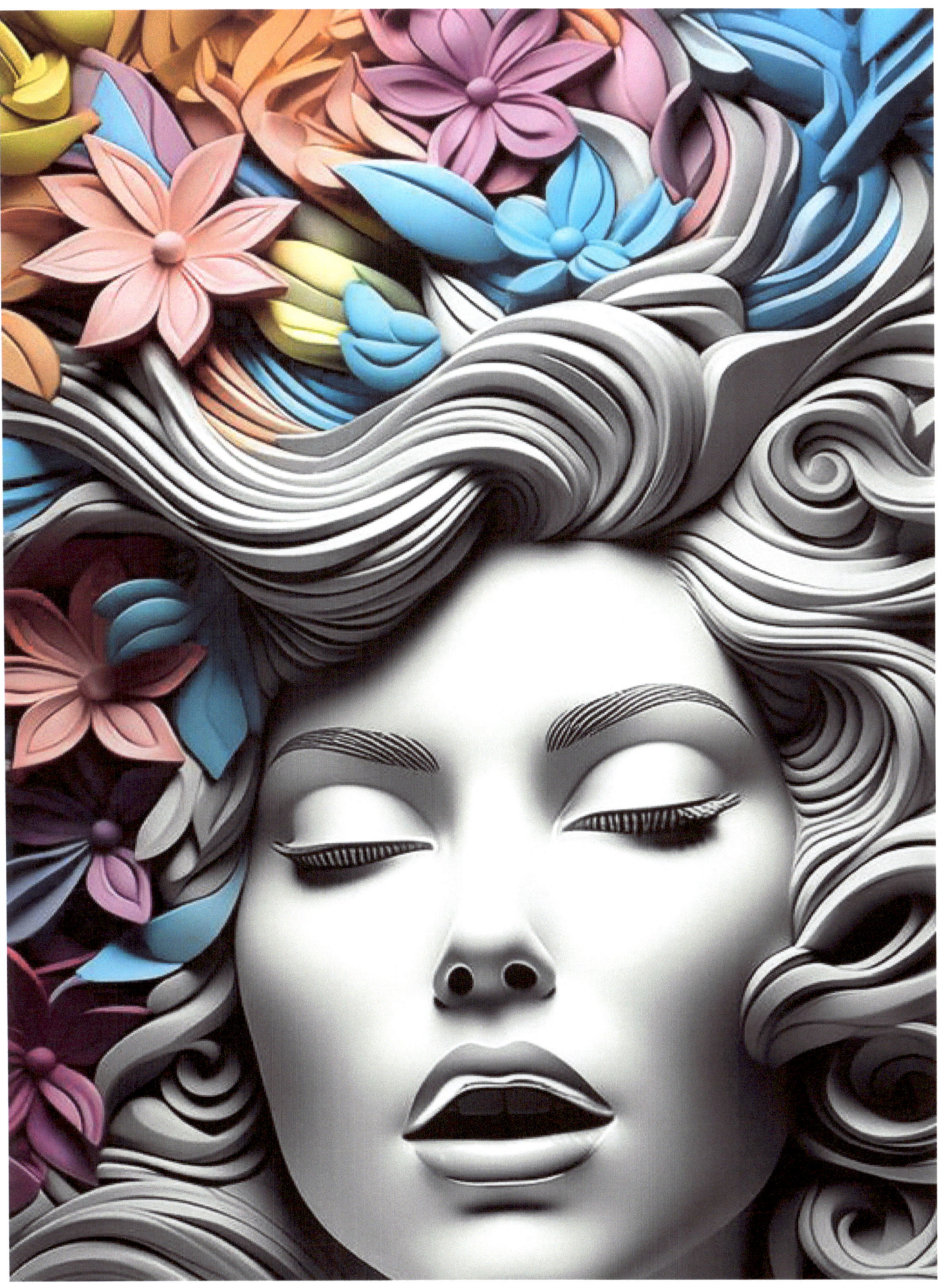

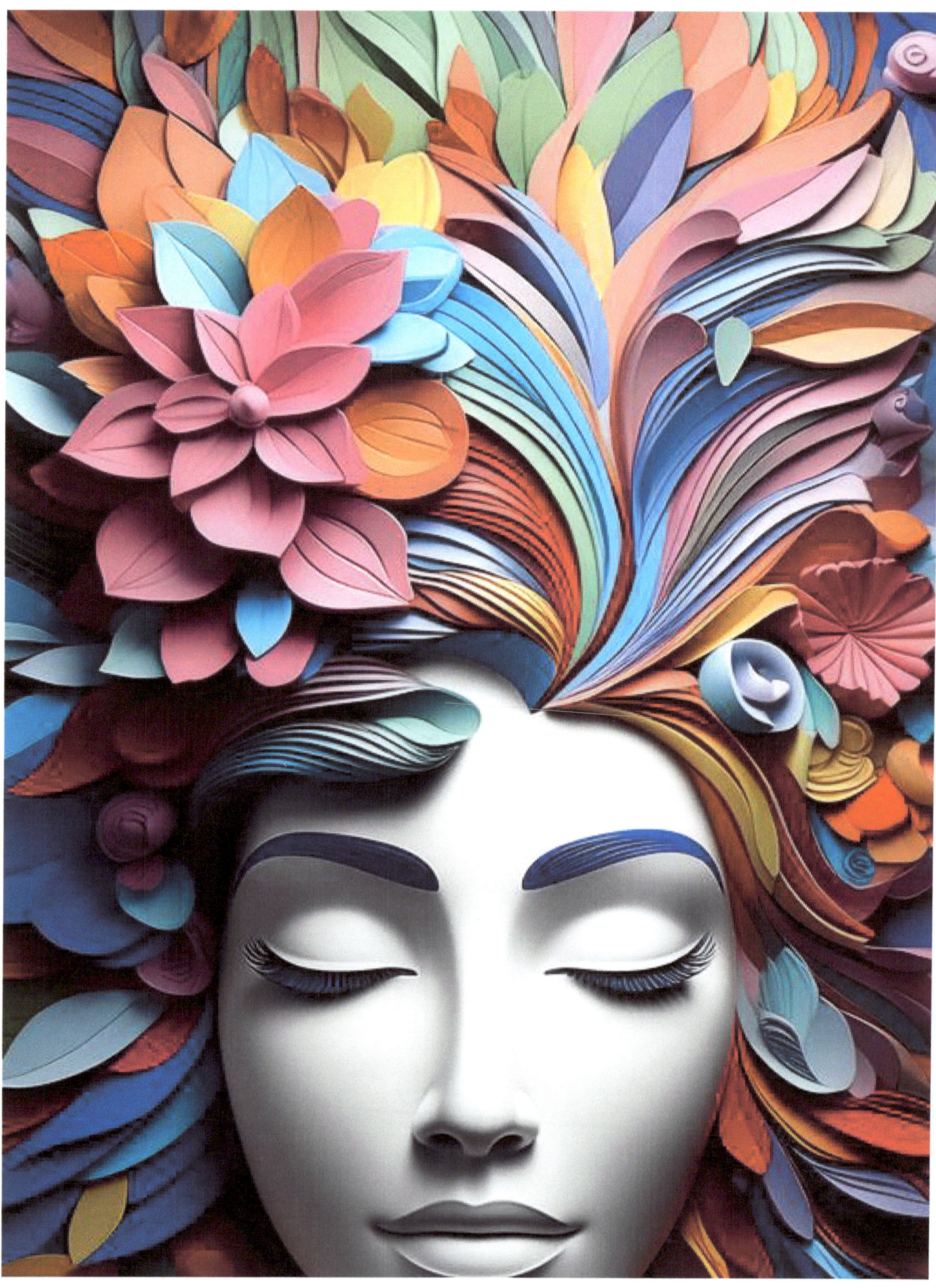

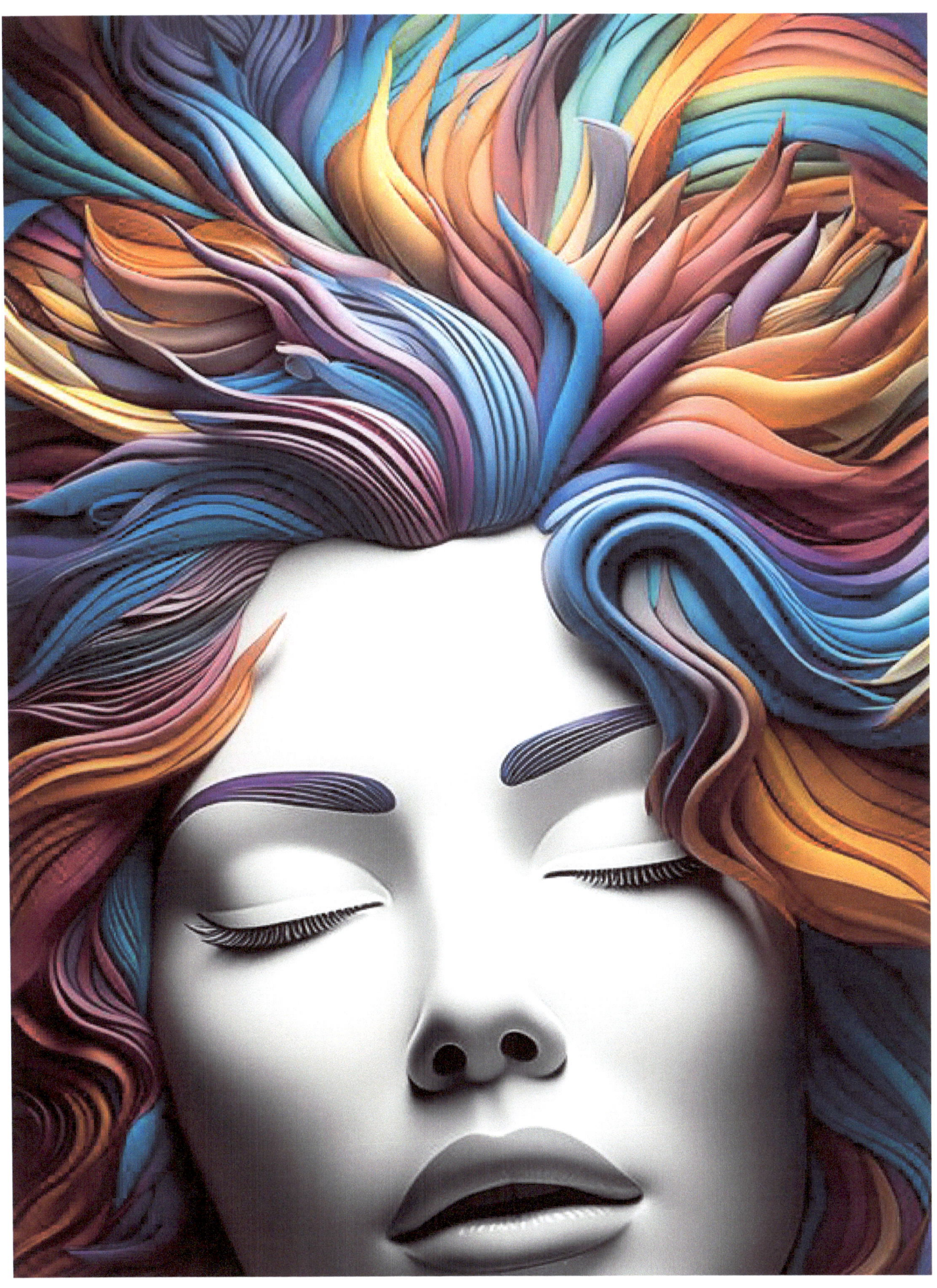

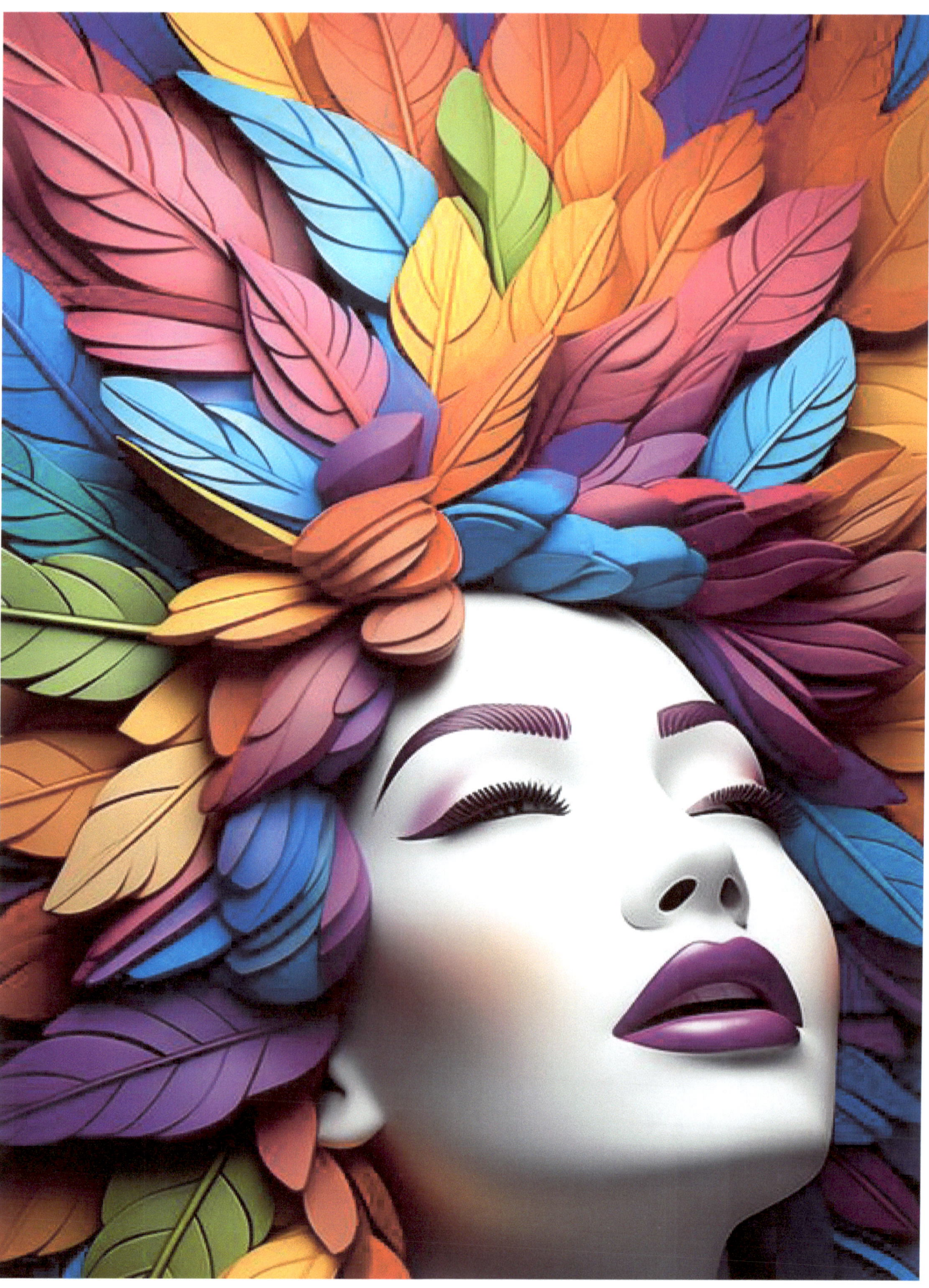

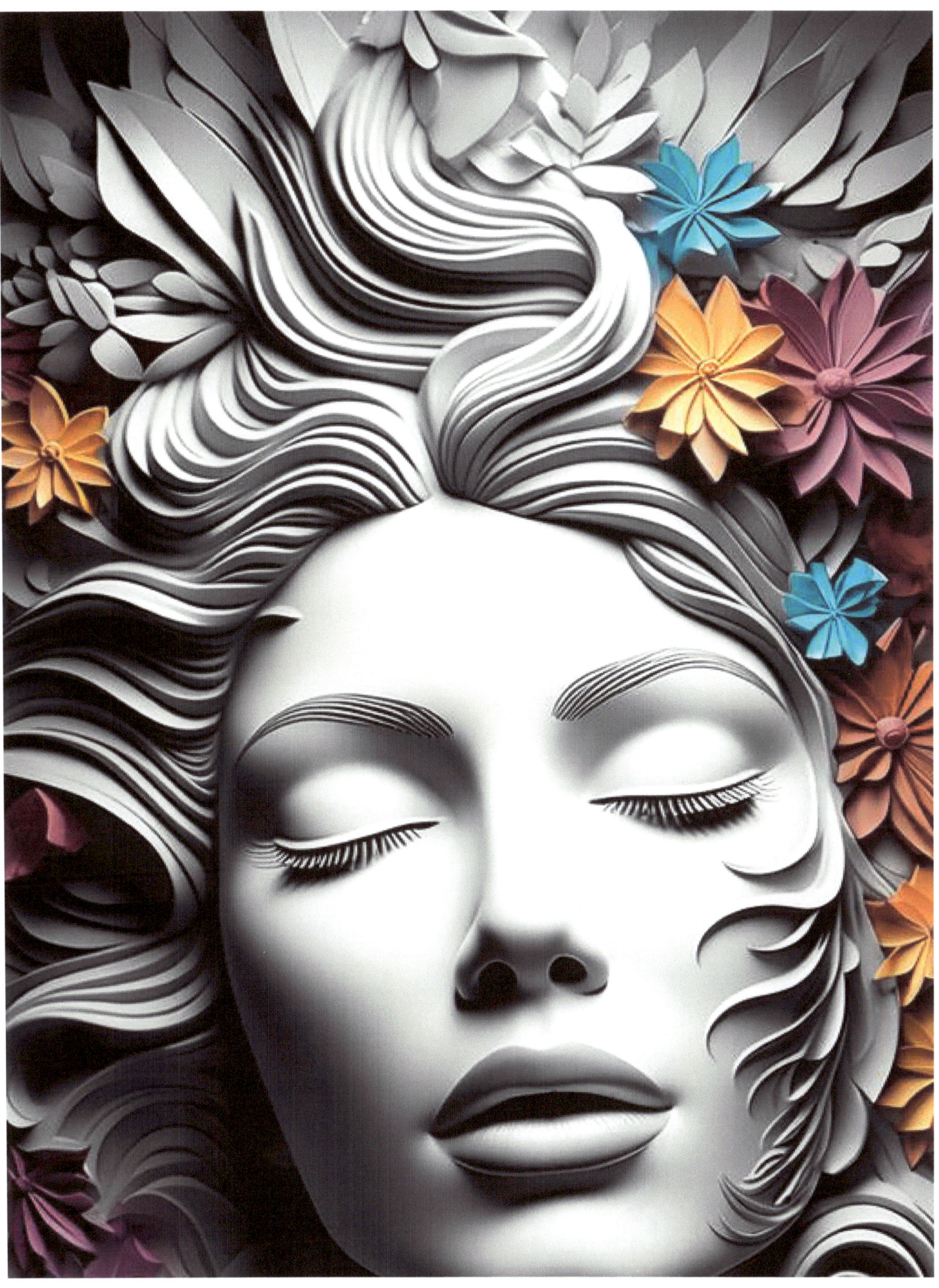

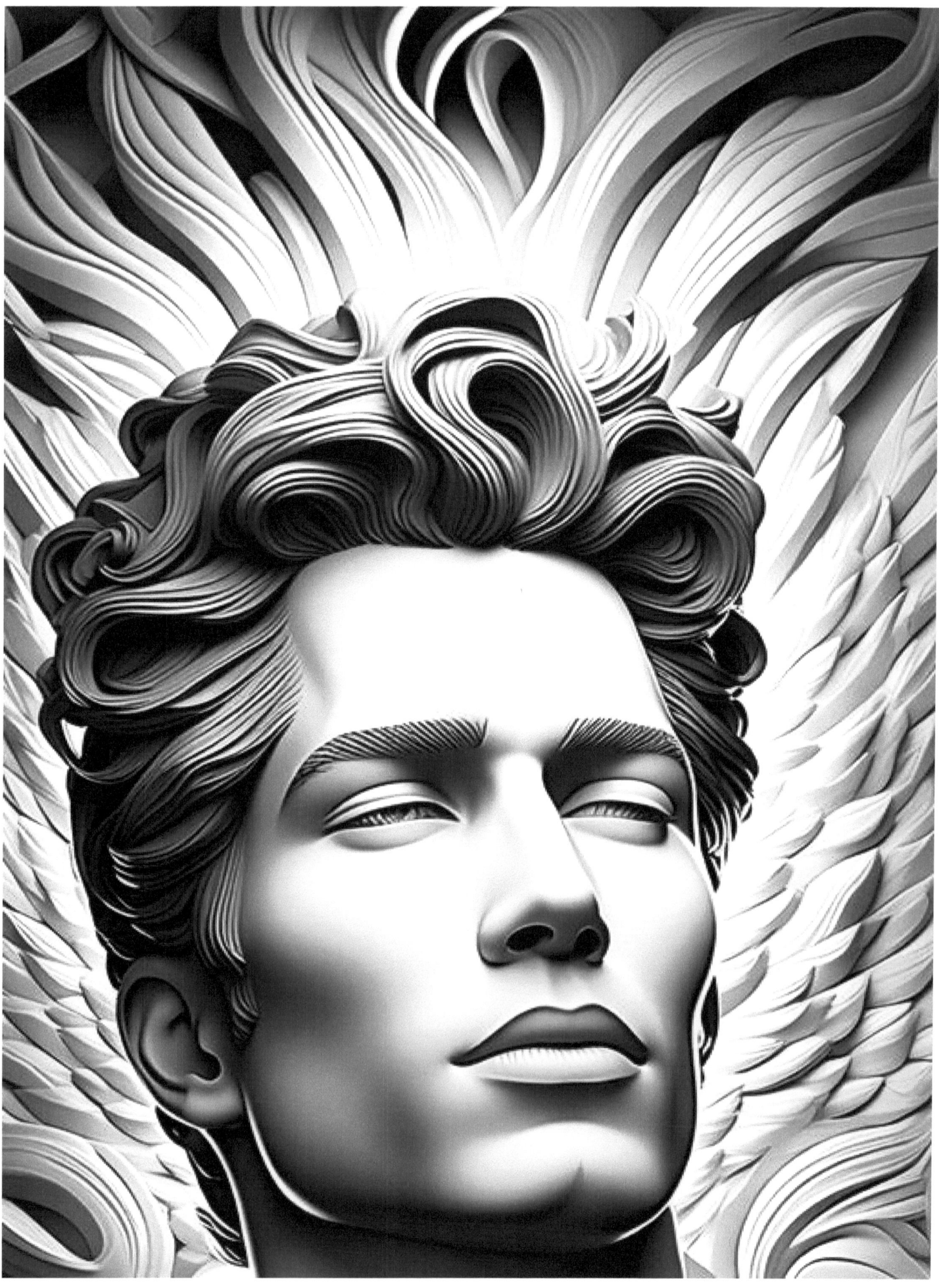

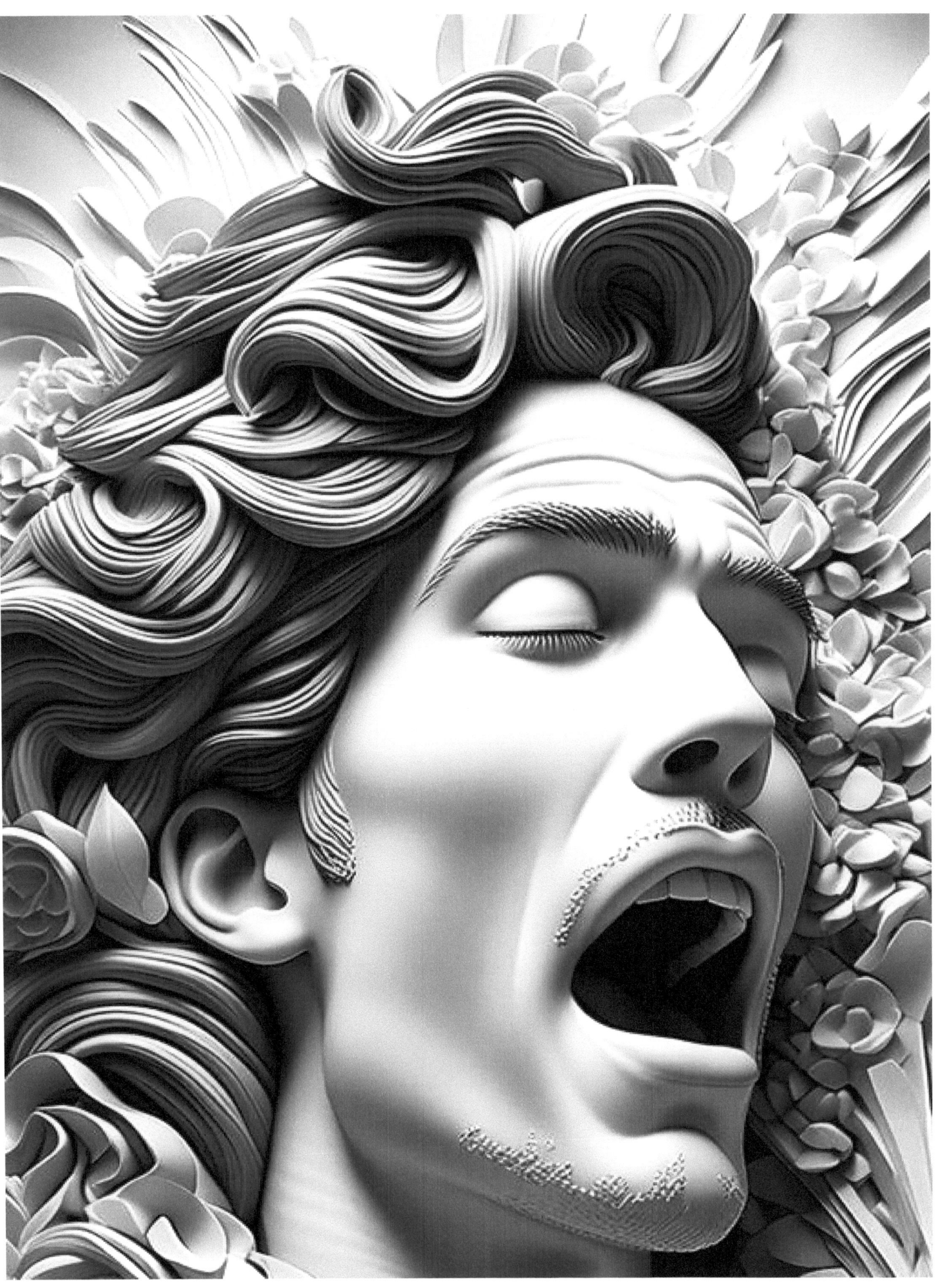

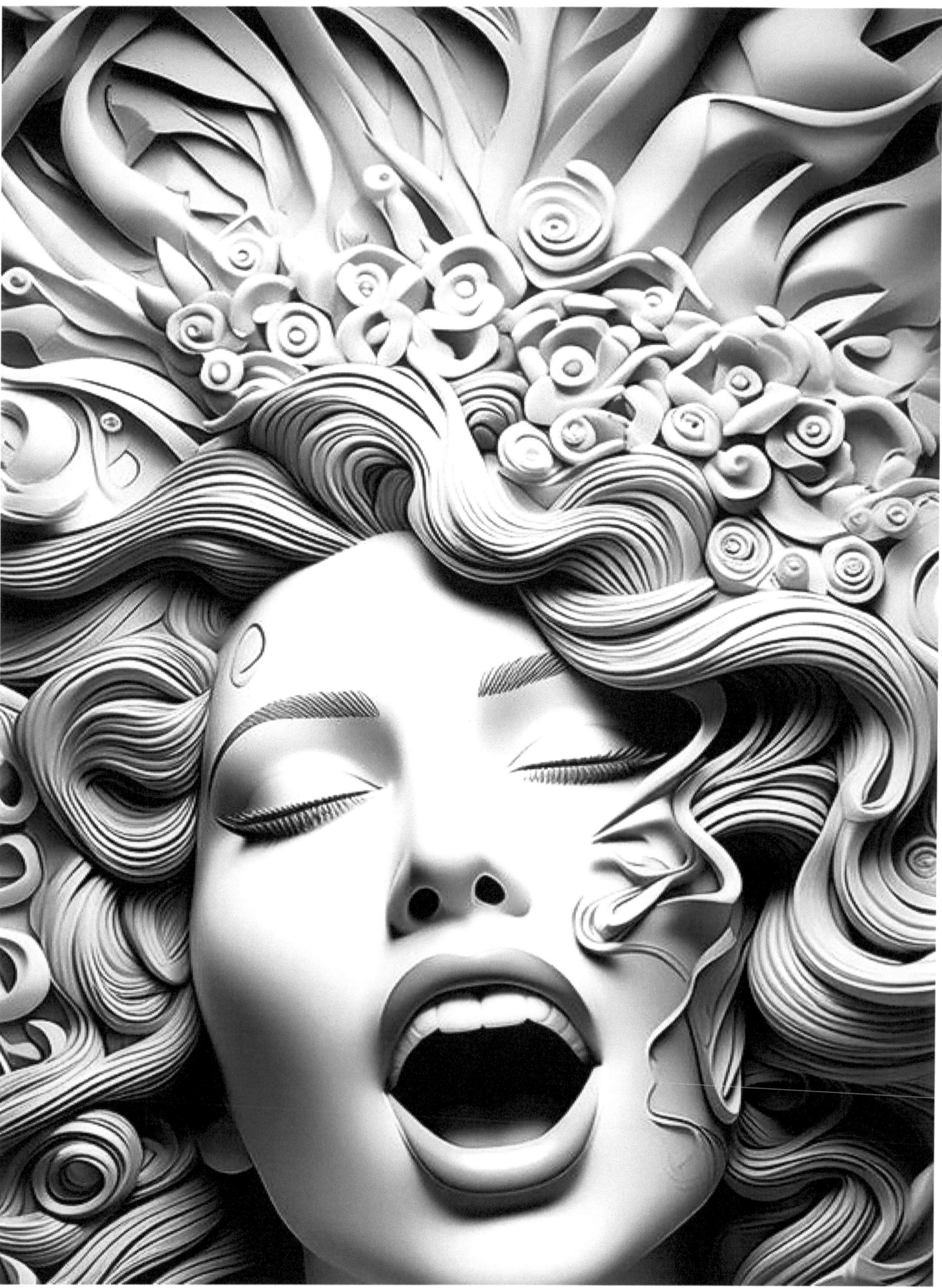

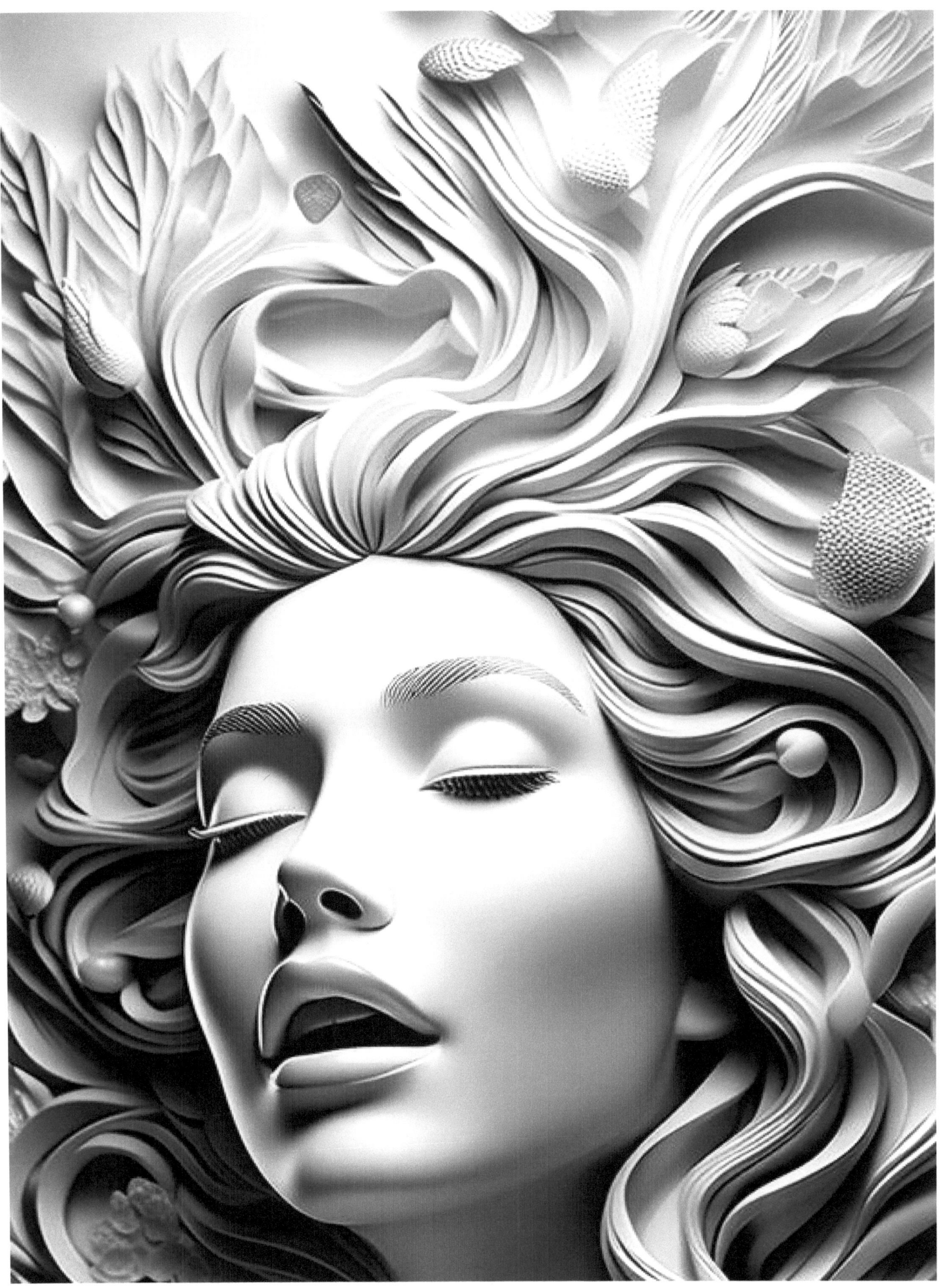

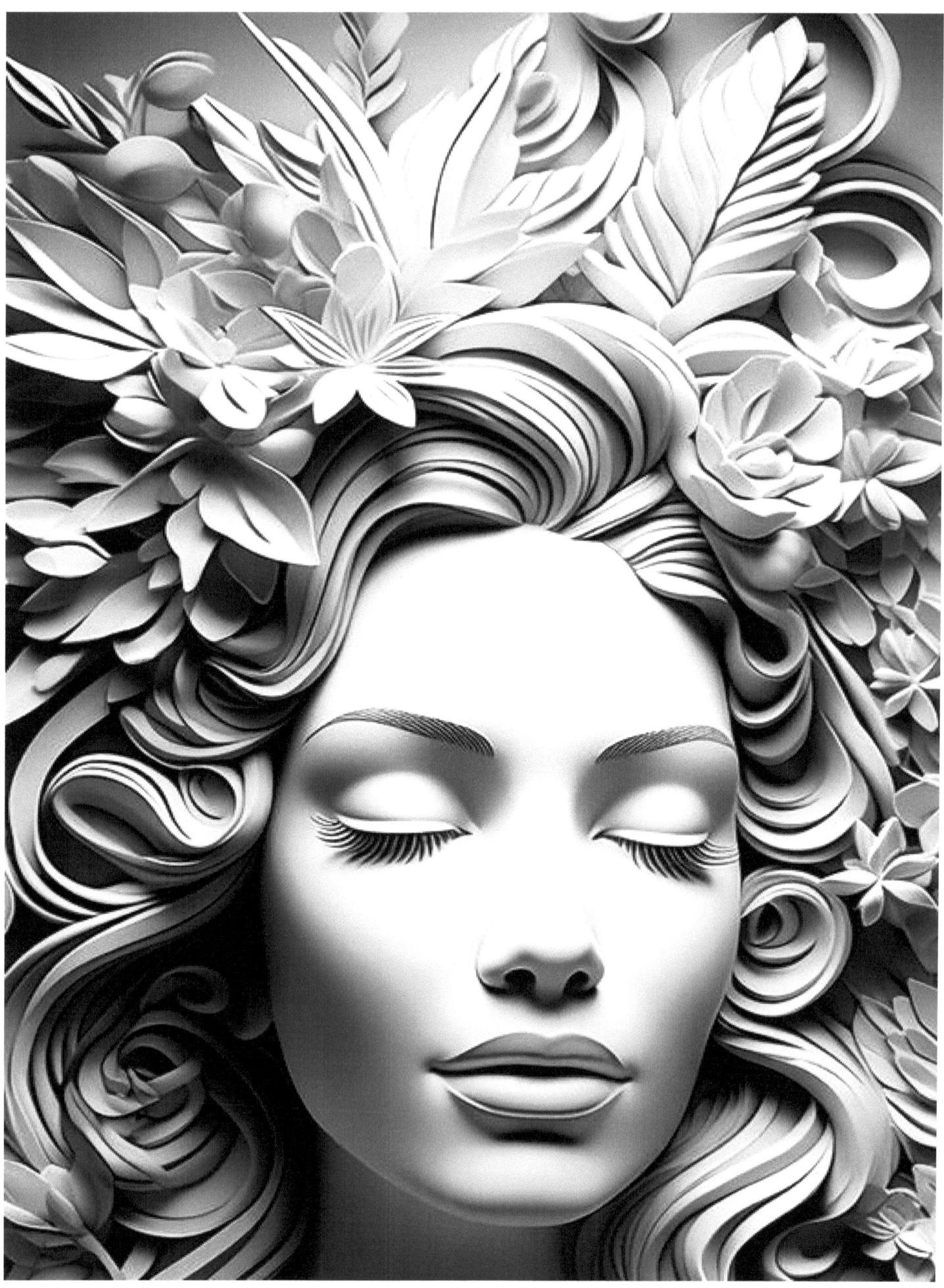

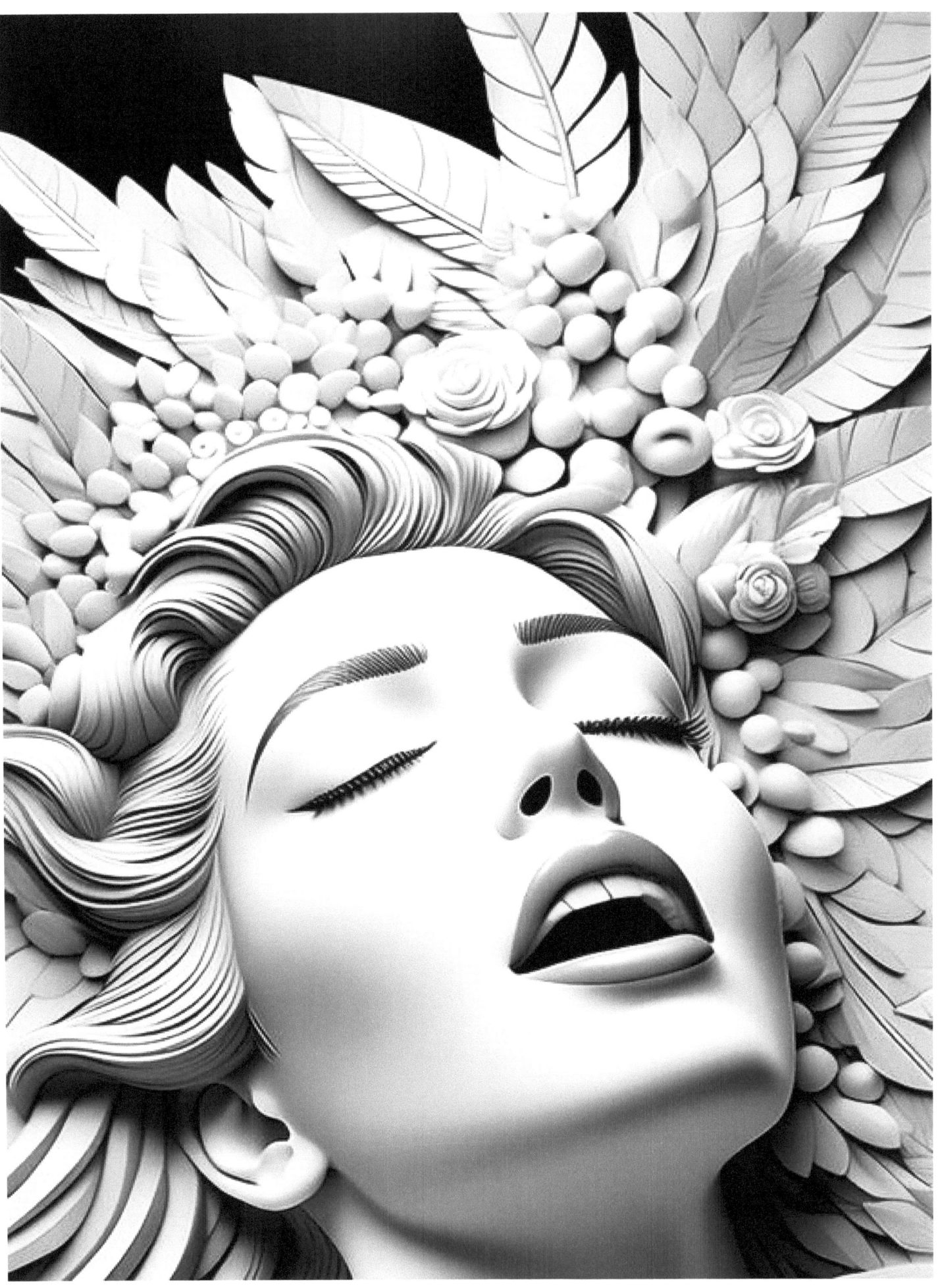

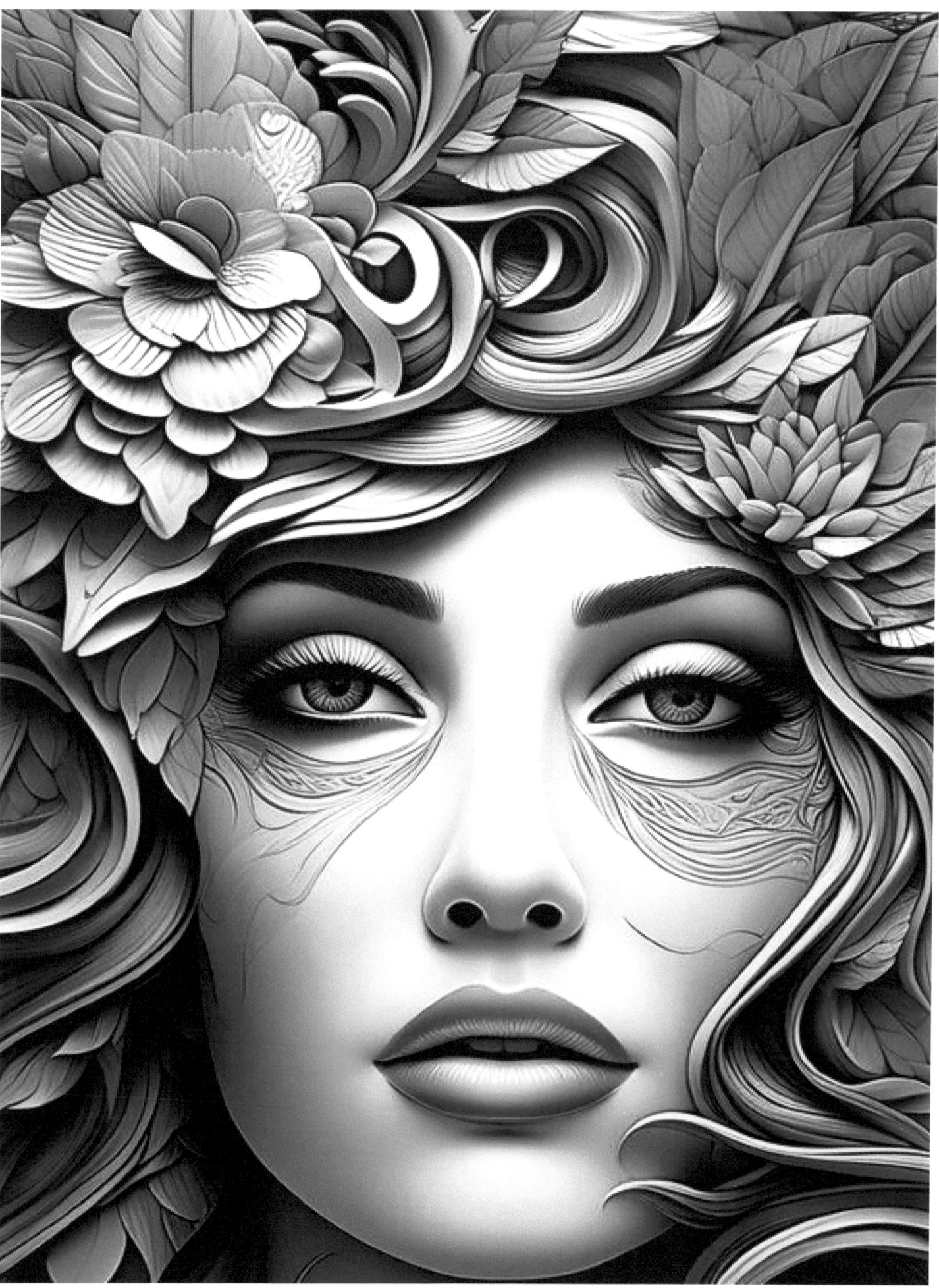

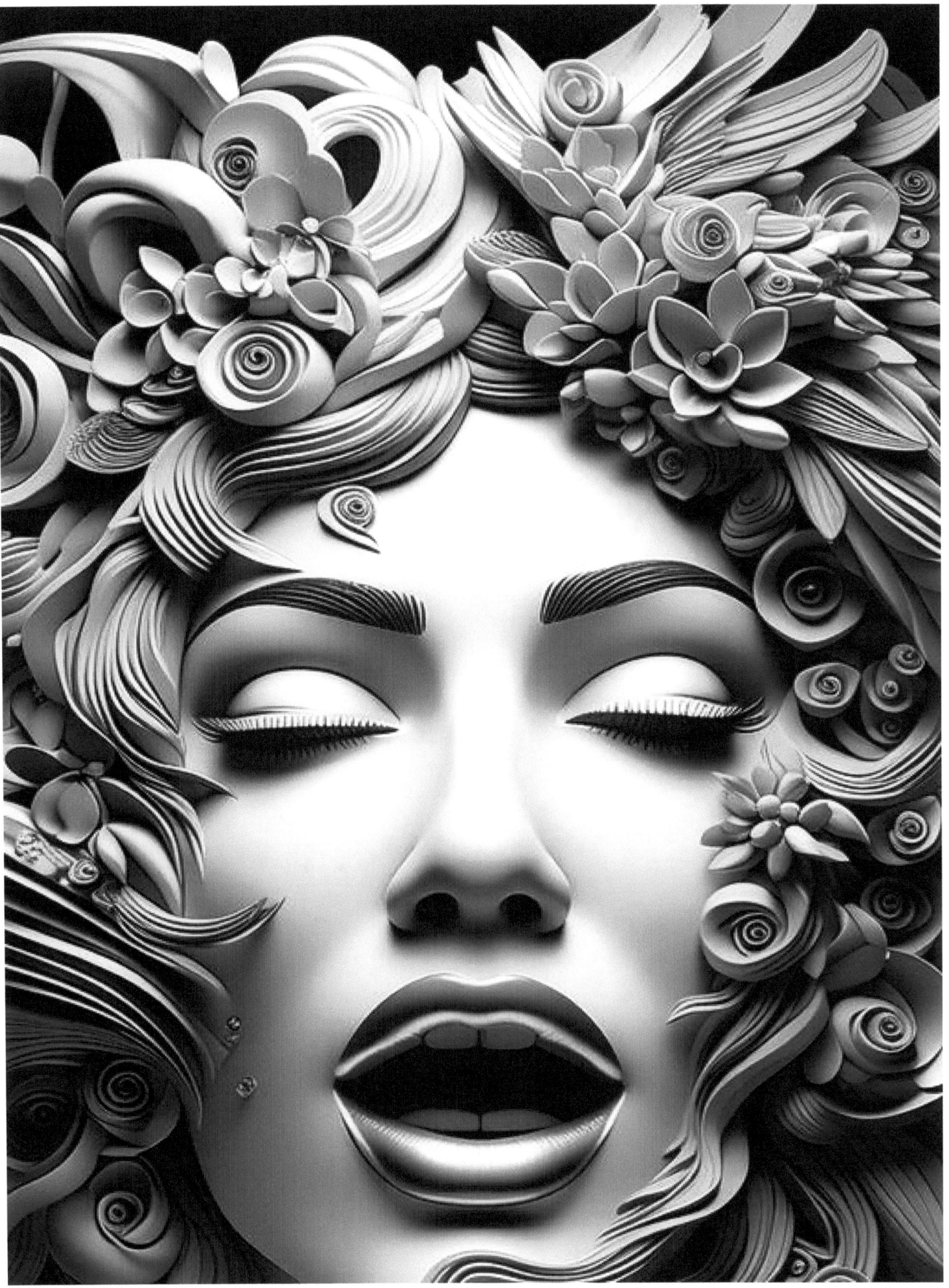

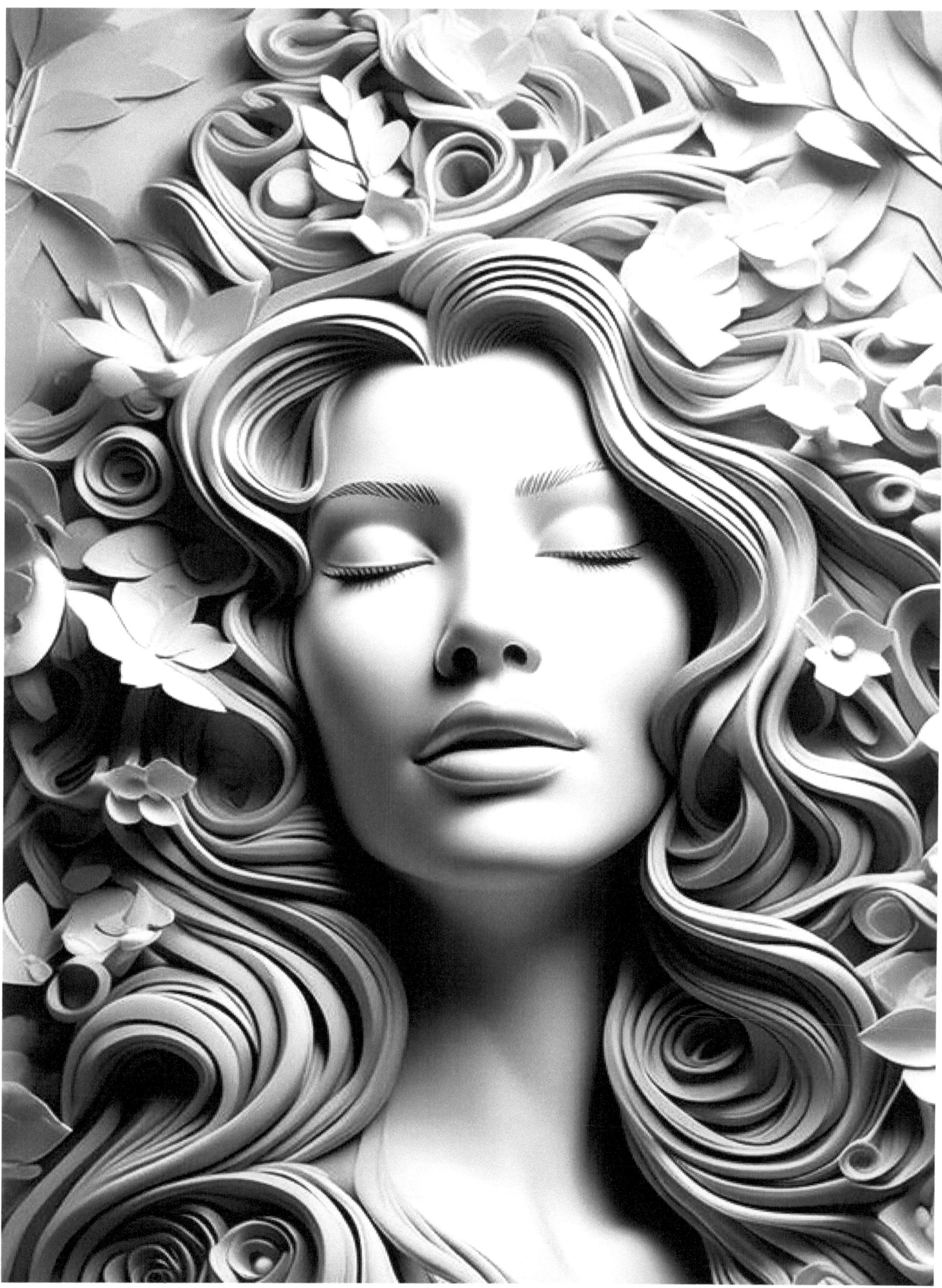

Thank you for choosing the Coffee Table Books
3D
Your support means the world to us. We hope our
book brings you endless joy and inspiration as you
fill its pages with your creativity. Happy coloring!

Warm regards,